WAR IN THE PACIFIC

PEARL HARBOR TO HIROSHIMA—THE PACIFIC WAR IN 400 COLOR PHOTOGRAPHS

WAR IN THE PACIFIC

PEARL HARBOR TO HIROSHIMA—THE PACIFIC WAR IN 400 COLOR PHOTOGRAPHS

Gina McNeely   Jon Guttman

METRO BOOKS
NEY YORK

Editorial Director: Will Steeds
Project Editor: Chris Stone
Designer: Philip Clucas
Copy Editor: Laura Pfost
Production: Robert Paulley
Proofreader: Julia North

Color reproduction: Modern Age Repro House Ltd,
Hong Kong

Metro Books
122 Fifth Avenue
New York, NY 10011

ISBN: 978-1-4351-3183-5

Printed and bound in China

10 9 8 7 6 5 4 3 2 1

Contents

Preface

Soon after its invention in 1839, the camera made its way onto—or at least near—the battlefield: during the Mexican-American War in 1846–48, in British wars in Burma and India in 1848–52, during the Russian invasion of Ottoman-held Romanian territory in 1853–55, during the Crimean War in 1855, and during the American Civil War of 1861–65. In World Wars I and II, film replaced the glass plate negative; film, lenses, and shutter speeds were faster; cameras were lighter and less bulky. All those developments gave the photographer the mobility and flexibility to keep up with the faster-moving events that attended twentieth-century warfare.

It was also during World War I that the first color photographs appeared, but they were expensive and time-consuming to produce. That aspect of photography had also advanced by World War II, though the amount of Kodachrome-type transparencies were still limited by expense and longer development time, their vulnerability to heat and other atmospheric conditions, and the relative difficulty in shipping them to facilities at home, such as the Rochester Institute of Technology in New York in the case of the Americans.

Those factors must be taken into consideration when surveying *War in the Pacific*. Since the United States and nations of the British Commonwealth were the only countries active in the Pacific Theater that had color photography at the time, images of the early Japanese conquests are rare (generally, they were the work of intrepid photojournalists for picture periodicals such as *Life* magazine.) With the widespread use of photographers attached to Allied military units and ships—as much for intelligence purposes as to preserve events for posterity—the amount of color photography increased in proportion to Allied success. In other words, the better the Allies were doing, the more color images became available.

War in the Pacific, then, cannot possibly be a comprehensive pictorial document of wartime events—for much of them, the images simply don't exist. Since the Japanese had virtually no color photography, they are represented, by and large, by whatever combat footage was taken of them, primarily documenting the worst of things as well as captured personnel and equipment.

Whenever possible, the author has tried to pick up the slack in the introductory narratives. Other than some context behind the pictures, they and the people captured in them are primarily left to speak for themselves.

Above: Japanese soldiers assault a Chinese position in the city of Teian, north of Kiukiang, terminus of the Nanchang Railway. Secured by the Japanese invaders on July 26, 1938, Kiukiang was part of the struggle for Hankow (now Wuhan), the largest battle of the Sino-Japanese "Incident" prior to World War II. After five months of fighting, Hankow finally fell to the Japanese on October 25.

Introduction

After choosing to open itself to contact with the United States and the European powers in 1871, Japan set itself on a course of emulating them by becoming an imperialist power in its own right—and then taking over their possessions and concessions in East Asia one by one, starting with Russia in 1905 and Germany in 1914. Hirohito, who rose to the throne as the Emperor Showa on December 25, 1926, encouraged a renewed Japanese militarism. This led to the invasion of Manchuria on September 19, 1931, and the establishment of a puppet regime in what the Japanese renamed Manchukuo in 1932. When the League of Nations condemned their act of aggression, the Japanese left it in March 1933.

In July 1937, the Japanese invaded China, where their atrocities against civilians shocked the outside world and set them on a collision course with the Western powers, particularly the United States, which imposed trade sanctions against shipments of strategic resources to sustain their war effort. Deeming a withdrawal from China unacceptable, Japan's militarists made ambitious plans to drive all Western powers from Asia and the Pacific, seizing their assets for themselves.

The question of where the Japanese would strike next was settled by an armed clash along the Manchukuo-Mongolian border that flared into undeclared war between Japanese and Soviet forces in August, ending in cease-fire on September 15 with the Japanese army defeated by Lieutenant General Georgy Zhukov. That setback led to the abandonment of the Japanese army's proposed "Northern Strategy" against the Soviet Union in favor of the navy-advocated "Southern Strategy" to seize the Asian and Pacific holdings of Britain, France, the Netherlands, and the United States.

Meanwhile, war had broken out in Europe as Nazi Germany invaded Poland in September 1939. France and Britain declared war on Germany, but could not prevent

Above: Adolf Hitler and Benito Mussolini ride through Rome during the German dictator's state visit on May 1, 1938. From 1939 to 1941, Hitler's war machine overran most of Western Europe, whereas Mussolini's attempts to revive the Roman Empire generally ended in embarrassing disaster, forcing the Nazi führer to divert valuable resources to bail his ally out, in Greece and North Africa.

> "We've got the power, we've got the instruments, we've got the agreement, we can do it . . . What the hell is Japan going to do?"
>
> —*Secretary of the Treasury Henry Morganthau, calling for an economic embargo on Japan in December 1937.*

Poland's dismemberment between the Germans and the Soviet Union, which had signed a nonaggression pact with Germany the month before. The Soviet Union invaded Finland on November 30, 1939, but suffered a string of embarrassing defeats before finally overpowering the Finns into ceding part of the Karelian Isthmus on March 13, 1940. On April 9, the Germans invaded

Denmark and Norway, followed on May 10 by Belgium, the Netherlands, and France. With France's surrender on June 23, only Britain remained to oppose Germany in the West, but it fended off a German aerial onslaught in the Battle of Britain, between July and October 1940.

Germany already had an ally in Fascist Italy, but on September 27, 1940, those two would-be powers acquired a third partner when Japan signed the Tripartite Pact in Berlin, creating a Rome-Berlin-Tokyo Axis. Since Italy entered the war against France on June 10, 1940, its October 28 invasion of Greece was thrown back, its forces in North Africa were routed by the British, and its battle fleet was crippled in Taranto Harbor on November 11 by British carrier-based torpedo bombers, whose techniques the Japanese studied for their own future use—starting with Pearl Harbor. In February 1941, Major General Erwin Rommel and a contingent of German desert troops, soon to be known as the Afrika Korps, arrived in Tripoli to rescue Italy's flagging fortunes in North Africa. Between April and late May 1941, the *Wehrmacht* overran Yugoslavia, Greece, and Crete.

Opposite: A 50mm antitank gun crew of a *Panzergrenadier* regiment eliminates a Red Army-held strongpoint during the German drive into the Soviet Union. Planned by Hitler as the ultimate culmination of his conquests throughout Europe, Germany's "Anti-Bolshevik Crusade," backed by contingents from Italy, Romania, Hungary, Slovakia, Croatia, and Finland, as well as volunteer units from Spain and Germany's captive nations, suffered its first setback at the very gates of Moscow in December 1941.

Above: A unit of Generalissimo Chiang Kai-shek's Nationalist Chinese Army, or Kuomintang, drills in 1940. Since 1937, the Chinese had suffered a succession of defeats at the hands of Japan's more consistently trained soldiers and advanced weaponry, but 1941 saw Chiang's government fighting on from its new capital of Chungking. Meanwhile, President Franklin D. Roosevelt had imposed trade sanctions on Japan until it withdrew from China—an option that the Japanese militarists regarded as unacceptable.

On June 22, 1941, German dictator Adolf Hitler turned on the Soviet Union in a massive invasion that almost reached Moscow before counterattacks, bolstered by reinforcements brought from Siberia, drove the Germans back on December 6. One reason the Soviets were able to remove troops from the Far East was because a German communist spying for the Soviets within the German legation in Tokyo, Richard Sorge, had sent them some critical information: Japan was about to strike at the western Allied powers in Asia and the Pacific. On December 7, Japan would prove that intelligence to be correct.

Chapter 1

Blazing Sun

Japan's Pacific rampage

Opposite: Boeing workers gather to hear a B-17 veteran's testimonial from Captain Hewitt T. Wheless of the 19th Bombardment Group. He received the Distinguished Flying Cross for attacking a Japanese landing force off Legaspi, Luzon, on December 14, 1941, and surviving a 75-mile (120.5km) running engagement with 12 enemy fighters to land at Cagayan with 1,200 bullet holes in his B-17D, two engines dead, one man killed, and three wounded.

Admiral Isoroku Yamamoto opposed war with the United States, whose military potential he understood from having visited that country. When Japan committed itself to that course of action, however, he dutifully sought to gain his country an early edge by planning an audacious aircraft carrier-launched surprise attack on the US Fleet at Pearl Harbor, Hawaii. Launched on December 7, 1941, the Pearl Harbor raid was devastating, but the fact that it occurred before the Japanese embassy received the order to declare war spurred the largely isolationist American populace to mobilize with a righteous vengeance. Moreover, although they crippled the American battleship fleet in the Pacific, the Japanese found no aircraft carriers at Pearl Harbor, they failed to destroy any of the four submarines berthed there, nor did they set fire to the fuel stocks—omissions they would later come to regret.

Nevertheless, for almost half a year the Japanese surge into Asia and the Pacific seemed irresistible. Hong Kong, Malaya, Singapore, and Burma fell, as did the Philippines, Guam, Wake Island, and the Netherlands East Indies. On February 19, 1942, the Japanese Combined Fleet raided Port Darwin, Australia, and in April it struck at Ceylon, driving Britain's Royal Navy from the eastern Indian Ocean and sinking *Hermes*, the first aircraft carrier to fall victim to carrier planes.

The first setback came in May 1942, when a Japanese attempt to land troops at Port Moresby, New Guinea, was repulsed in the Battle of the Coral Sea. A more dramatic turn of events occurred at Midway Island on June 4, when US Navy dive bombers sank four aircraft carriers. Although the Americans lost a carrier and a destroyer of their own at Midway, they had handed the Japanese their first naval defeat in 350 years and, more important, robbed them at last of their offensive momentum.

"A military man can scarcely pride himself on having smitten a sleeping enemy; it is more a matter of shame, simply, for the one smitten."

—*Admiral Isoroku Yamamoto, on the success of the Pearl Harbor attack on December 7, 1941.*

Isoroku Yamamoto (1884–1943)

Born Isoroku Takano, Japan's leading naval strategist graduated from the Imperial Naval Academy in 1904 and lost two fingers of his left hand on May 25, 1905, while serving aboard the cruiser *Nisshin* in the decisive victory over the Russian fleet at Tsushima Strait. Adopted in 1916 by the Yamamoto family, taking that as his surname, he studied at Harvard University in 1919–21 and served as naval attaché in Washington, DC. Amid the militarism that dominated the Japanese army, Yamamoto opposed the invasion of China and war with the United States, and regarded the Tripartite Pact with Germany and Italy as "against Japan's natural interests." Once his country was committed to war, however, Yamamoto loyally devoted himself to seeking a victory that he personally regarded as a long shot.

Opposite: A North American SNJ-1, resplendent in prewar US Navy markings, performs a training flight in 1941. The SNJ and its Army Air Corps cousin, the AT-6, were the most ubiquitous advanced trainers in all American services, with an export model, the Harvard, also serving the British Royal Air Force and the Royal Canadian Air Force. They prepared a vital first line of airmen for the world war to come, as well as for the generations to follow.

Right: The instructor aboard an SNJ-1 snaps a photograph of the destroyer *Drayton* (DD-366) off the American West Coast in October 1941. Laid down in 1934 and completed in 1936, *Drayton* was one of the *Mahan* class, part of a general modernization program in the US Navy. Nicknamed the "Blue Beetle" for its prewar camouflage scheme, *Drayton* earned 11 battle stars in the course of its long wartime service, including the Battle of Tassafaronga on November 30, 1942, after which it rescued 128 crewmen from the sunken heavy cruiser *Northampton*.

Right: Filipinos examine a partially assembled Seversky P-35A of the 17th Pursuit Squadron on Luzon. The P-35A was based on the export model EP-106, 60 of which were sold to Sweden before the United States imposed a weapons embargo, excluding only Great Britain, in June 1940. Of the 60 P-35As impounded, 57 were sent to the Philippines, where 48 were serving with the 17th and 34th Pursuit Squadrons when the Japanese attacked.

November 18–December 30, 1941: *In Operation Crusader, the Eighth Army wins Britain's first major land victory over the Germans, driving Erwin Rommel's forces back to El Agheila and taking Bardia, Sollum, and Halfaya.*

January 16, 1942: *Rommel launches a "reconnaissance in force" out of El Agheila and, finding advance Eighth Army elements scattered, counterattacks in force to drive the British back to Gazala, where both sides will remain stalemated until May.*

Right: Among the US Army Air Corps contingent in Hawaii were 33 Douglas B-18A Bolo bombers of the 5th and 11th Bomb Groups, most of which were destroyed on the ground in the Japanese attack. Initially thought adequate to handle the Japanese threat, the obsolescent B-18 was swiftly withdrawn from Pacific service and relegated to antisubmarine patrol work in the Caribbean Sea, defending merchant shipping against German U-boats.

Left: On December 7, 1941, Japanese carrier planes staged a surprise attack on the US Fleet at Pearl Harbor, Hawaii. The eight battleships sunk or damaged included *West Virginia* (foreground) and *Tennessee*, but only *Arizona* and *Oklahoma* were permanently lost. The United States declared war on Japan the next day, and on the eleventh, Adolf Hitler declared war on the United States.

Above: Struck by a converted artillery shell dropped from a Japanese Nakajima B5N2 torpedo bomber, battleship *Arizona* explodes in the only color photograph taken of its demise. Of the 2,404 Americans killed in the Pearl Harbor raid, 1,177 died aboard *Arizona*. Battleship *Oklahoma* capsized and, although raised, was scrapped rather than repaired and modernized like the other six battleships that were sunk or damaged.

February–March 1942: *The German naval campaign to disrupt Allied shipping in the Atlantic grows with the United States' entry into the war, with a slaughter that U-boat crews call the "Second Happy Time."*

April 24, 1942: *Spring thaws render the "Road of Life" across the ice of Lake Ladoga—by which evacuation and supply transport had been keeping Leningrad alive since November 10, 1941—inoperable, cutting off the city until December 20.*

"They wanted this war and yet they did not want it. They talked about it all the time, out of bravado and in imitation of their leaders, but they never really believed in it . . . Tokyo is afraid, the Japanese are panic-stricken by their own daring."

—Vichy French journalist Robert Guillain, from Tokyo, December 8, 1941.

Above: Crippled at Pearl Harbor, the battleship *West Virginia* underwent preliminary repairs and is shown on April 30, 1943, ready to depart for Puget Sound Navy Yard, Washington, DC, for more thorough work including upgraded radar and other equipment. A newer generation battleship, probably *North Carolina*, lies at the far end of the pier. *West Virginia*'s eight 16-inch (40.5cm) guns would help sink the Japanese battleship *Yamashiro* during the Battle of Surigao Strait on October 24, 1944.

Right: A Seversky P-35A of the 34th Pursuit Squadron on its nose on Del Carmen airfield. Catching the Americans by surprise in their initial onslaught on December 8, the Formosa-based Japanese planes destroyed most of their aircraft over the next few days. Only eight P-35s remained airworthy by December 12, but their desperate crews kept some of them flying and fighting until May 1942.

Left: Marines parade in San Diego, California, in early 1942. The small marine garrison on Wake Island added to the corps' traditions on December 11, 1941, when it turned back an amphibious landing for the only time in the war, while its shore gunners sank the Japanese destroyer *Hayate*, and one of its Grumman F4F-3s sank the destroyer *Kisaragi*. On December 23, however, a renewed Japanese effort, supported by carriers *Soryu* and *Hiryu*, overwhelmed Wake's defenders.

Above: A mother reads a letter from one of her four sons who enlisted "for the duration," under flags that suggest that they chose the same branch of service. After the deaths of all five of the Sullivan brothers aboard the light cruiser *Juneau* on the night of November 13–14, 1942, the US military made a policy of not assigning any related personnel to the same unit.

"Enemy on island issue in doubt."

—Radio message from Commander Winfield Scott Cunningham from Wake Island, which had repulsed a Japanese invasion attempt on December 11, on a second landing on December 23. Cunningham surrendered his overwhelmed garrison half an hour later.

Internment at Tule Lake

Pearl Harbor raised a popular antipathy toward Japanese Americans that was much harsher than that held toward Americans of German or Italian descent. In February 1942, the Roosevelt administration ordered the relocation of Japanese Americans to internment camps, such as the Tule Lake Relocation Center at Newell, California.

Few challenged the incarceration, ostensibly for their own "protection," of some 100,000 Japanese Americans. But the internees themselves often demonstrated in protest of unsanitary living conditions, inadequate medical care, poor food, and unsafe working conditions, climaxing in November 1943, when the US Army imposed martial law over the camp. Some were relocated to higher-security "concentration camps," such as those at Heart Mountain, Wyoming, and Topaz, Utah. Even while undergoing suspicion and scathing bigotry, Japanese Americans struggled to serve the country. One, Ben Kuroki from Nebraska, became a bomber gunner, his 30 missions in Consolidated B-24Ds including the August 1, 1943, Ploesti raid, followed by another 28 over Japan in Boeing B-29s. Finally Roosevelt, following his reelection in November 1944, canceled the "War Emergency Evacuation" and closed the camps.

Above: The scene from a nearby hillside of Tule Lake Relocation Center. The facility held Japanese Americans who, usually due to confusion over its intent, had failed to take an oath of "undivided loyalty" to the United States.

Left: Japanese American internees at the Tule Lake Relocation Center put on their best faces for the camera.

Opposite: Internees plant cucumbers at the Tule Lake Relocation Center.

Left: Charles Fenno Jacobs of Edward Steichen's Naval Aviation Photographic Unit took this picture of aviation cadets filling out the necessary paperwork beside their SNJ-3 during training at a naval air station. The US Navy's training program, like the Army Air Corps—soon redesignated the Army Air Forces—underwent rapid, exponential expansion to meet the challenge of a total war on two major fronts.

Opposite top: Robert T. Smith, an ace of the American Volunteer Group with one of its Curtiss 81-A-2s (export P-40Bs). Amid general Allied disaster, the AVG, or "Flying Tigers," under Colonel Claire L. Chennault's brilliant tactical leadership, claimed 297 enemy planes destroyed for the loss of 21 men killed or captured. Between May 7 and 10, 1942, eight of its fighters bombed, strafed, and ultimately drove a Japanese division back from the Salween River Gorge, preventing an invasion of China from the south.

Opposite: Trainers in transition: Aircrews of the First Marine Aircraft Wing, in a North American SNJ-3 (foreground) and a Curtiss SBC-4 dive bomber, fly in formation in the spring of 1942. Unofficially known as the Helldiver—the second of three dive bombers to bear that name—the SBC-4 was the last biplane accepted by the US Navy and continued on in the training role into the summer of 1943.

Left: F. W. "Mike" Hunter, a US Army Air Forces test pilot at the Douglas plant in Long Beach, California, poses before one of the company's products in October 1942. Developed by the Shure Brothers Company and adopted by the USAAF in 1942, Hunter's T-30 throat microphone was held over the larynx by a rubber band, freeing the airman's hands while enabling clearer transmission over outside noise.

Opposite: The American war effort, already underway for national defense and to provide weapons and supplies to Britain, the Commonwealth, and Allies in exile through the Lend-Lease program, went into overdrive after Pearl Harbor, as the United States faced the prospect of what amounted to two separate, very different conflicts in Europe and the Far East. A succession of B-25B Mitchell bombers emerge from the North American assembly line in 1942.

Below: A riveting team works on the cockpit shell of a C-47 at the plant of North American Aviation Inc. in Inglewood, California, which was license-producing the Douglas-designed transports. The need to free up manpower for the armed forces led to women playing a growing role in the factories. Toward that end, "Rosie the Riveter's" contribution was vital; her influence on women's postwar place in American society would be profound.

Alfred T. Palmer (1906–1993)

Born in San Francisco, California, Alfred T. Palmer was one month old when the city was devastated by an earthquake—which his father photographed. He worked for Ansel Adams in 1916, and in 1932 he became the Dollar Lines' official photographer. His job and wanderlust would carry him around the world 23 times in 32 years. When President Franklin D. Roosevelt formed the Office of War Information in June 1940, Palmer became the head of its photography department from 1941 to 1943. One of his signature techniques was to use a crude interior lighting method that highlighted his human subjects. His photographs on these pages show factory production on the West Coast in the war's early months.

Above: Recruits train on coastal artillery at Camp Collan, near San Diego, on January 1, 1942. Californians took such practice seriously after December 20, 1941, when Japanese submarine *I-17* forced the 6,912-ton (6,270 tonnes) tanker *Emidio* to run aground off Crescent City. On February 23, 1942, *I-17* attacked the Richfield aviation fuel tanks west of Santa Barbara, causing little damage but earning notoriety as the first Axis ship to shell the American mainland.

Left: "Seabees" of a US Navy construction battalion emplace one of seven 7-inch (18cm) guns on a hilltop overlooking Teavanui Harbor on Bora Bora after the uncontested landing of 5,000 American troops on the Vichy French possession on February 17, 1942. The Seabees also built a seaplane base and an airfield that served as the Society Islands' only means of air transport for years after Bora Bora was returned to the French on June 2, 1946.

Admiral Ernest J. King (1887–1956)

On December, 30, 1941, Admiral Ernest Joseph King was appointed commander in chief of the US Fleet, and on March 18, 1942, he became commander of naval operations, the only officer to hold both posts simultaneously. Although supportive of President Franklin D. Roosevelt's "Germany First" policy, the abrasively outspoken King was adamant about allocating suitable naval assets for the war against Japan. He also opposed the Royal Navy's return into the Pacific, which he regarded as an American theater of operations. Promoted to the rarely attained five-star rank of fleet admiral on December 17, 1944, King died of a heart attack on June 25, 1956.

"When I reflect how I have longed and prayed for the entry of the United States into the war, I find it difficult to realize how gravely our British affairs have deteriorated since December 7th."

—*Prime Minister Winston Churchill, on British defeats in Malaya, Burma, and the Indian Ocean by mid-April 1942.*

Above: The carrier *Enterprise*, shown in June 1941, was not at Pearl Harbor during the December 7 raid, though it lost seven aircraft there. On December 10, its planes caught Japanese submarine *I-70* reconnoitering the area and sank it. On February 1, *Enterprise* served as the nucleus of Task Force 8 as it conducted the first American counterstrike against Roi, Wotke, and Taroa in the Marshall Islands, sinking a transport and two smaller craft.

May 9, 1942: *After ferrying 47 Supermarine Spitfires to Malta on April 20—only for German attacks to destroy all of them within 48 hours—carrier USS* Wasp *and HMS* Eagle *deliver another critically needed 67 Spitfires to the island.*

May 12–28, 1942: *Marshal Semyon Timoshenko's offensive in the Kharkov region creates a salient that allows counterattacking German Generals Fedor von Bock and Friedrich Paulus to entrap and kill or capture more than 200,000 Soviet troops.*

"It was one of those plans which are called 'brilliant' if they succeed and 'foolhardy' if they fail."

—*Vice Admiral William F. Halsey, on the Marshall Islands raid on February 1, 1942.*

Above: Cooks perform their duties aboard a US Navy cruiser. While *Enterprise*'s planes worked over the Marshalls, Rear Admiral Raymond A. Spruance's heavy cruisers *Northampton* and *Salt Lake City* bombarded Wotje Atoll, and heavy cruiser *Chester* struck at Taroa. *Enterprise* lost one fighter and five dive bombers while claiming three Japanese fighters, whereas the Taroa-based Chitose *Kokutai* claimed 17 victories at a cost of one plane lost.

May 30–31, 1942: *Air Marshal Arthur Harris dispatches 1,047 bombers to the city of Cologne. Forty planes are lost in the first "Thousand Bomber Raid," the prelude to numerous future night attacks on German cities by RAF Bomber Command.*

June–July 1942: *Germans launch offensive into Caucasus Mountains and drive toward Stalingrad. Rommel wins Battle of Gazala, takes Tobruk, and drives into Egypt toward Alexandria until stopped at El Alamein between July 1 and 27.*

Opposite: Ensign Edward H. "Butch" O'Hare, the US Navy's first ace and its first pilot to be awarded the Medal of Honor during World War II, poses beside a Grumman F4F Wildcat. As carrier *Lexington* approached the new Japanese base at Rabaul, New Britain, it was attacked by 17 Mitsubishi G4M1s of the 4th *Kokutai* (naval air group). Although *Lexington*'s F4F-3s shot down or badly damaged 16 of the bombers— five credited to O'Hare—the raid was canceled.

Right: Pilot Don Downie chats with one of the thousands of Chinese coolies who built and maintained the runways on the Chinese terminus of the Hump. On January 29, 1944, Air Transport Command became the first noncombat organization to be awarded the Presidential Unit Citation for the efforts and sacrifices of its personnel. By August 1945, when operations wound down, the Hump crews had airlifted 650,000 tons (589,670 tonnes) of vitally needed supplies to China.

Thunder Down Under

Australian and New Zealand military personnel had been involved in the Pacific War since Japanese troops landed on Malaya on December 7, 1941. For Australians, the war suddenly veered closer to home on February 19, 1942, when 242 planes from carriers *Akagi, Kaga, Soryu,* and *Hiryu,* as well as land-based bombers, struck at Port Darwin in Northern Australia, sinking eight ships, destroying 23 aircraft, and killing at least 297 people. Australia would suffer almost 100 further air raids until November 1943.

Japan's invasion of northern Papua New Guinea and its march on Port Moresby also posed a threat that Australians could not ignore. They also became heavily engaged in the Solomon Islands, as did soldiers, sailors, and airmen of New Zealand. Ironically, most of the 3,600 Maoris who volunteered to defend their homeland served with the 28th (Maori) Brigade in North Africa, Italy, and Greece, where 649 were killed and 1,712 wounded. Others, however, worked on the home front, with postwar social consequences in New Zealand similar to those attending blacks and women contributing to the war effort in the United States.

Right: HMNZS *Manuka*, one of four 540-ton (490 tonnes) *Castle*-class minesweepers built in New Zealand using wood in place of steel to conserve the latter commodity—and christened, appropriately, for the Maori word for a species of tree—is launched on April 4, 1942. After defending New Zealand's coastal waters throughout the war, *Manuka* was leased to the Chatham Fishing Company, a firm established by veteran servicemen returning home.

Opposite bottom: Maori volunteers in the New Zealand army stand for inspection on April 4, 1942. Most fought in North Africa and Europe, but others, working on the home front, more than doubled the percentage of Maoris in cities, thereby accelerating their assimilation into New Zealand society.

H.M.S. MANUKA

Above: Commonwealth Wackett and Wirraway trainers are assembled in Victoria in 1942. Cut off from Britain and awaiting American reinforcements, the Australians modified their Wirraway into a light bomber and even into a single-seat fighter, the Boomerang, which excelled as a close support ground strafer over New Guinea.

Left: Canadian servicewomen of various branches converse outside of a recruiting station in Vancouver, British Columbia. Canada was already fighting alongside Britain against Nazi Germany when it diverted some of its efforts toward guarding the west coast against Japan. By 1944, more than a million women were in Canada's full-time workforce—double what it had been in 1939—and Canadian women were also serving as military drivers, mechanics, nurses, aides, and pilots.

> "I claim we got a hell of a beating. We got run out of Burma, and it is humiliating as hell. I think we ought to find out what caused it, go back and retake it."

—Lieutenant General Joseph Stilwell, to news reporters in New Delhi on May 24, 1942.

Above: Second Lieutenant Benjamin F. Duke of the 8th Squadron, 49th Fighter Group, confers with his crew chief from the cockpit of his Curtiss P-40E under camouflage netting at Strauss Airstrip outside of Darwin in May 1942. Flying its first missions in Australia's defense, the 49th Group later distinguished itself over New Guinea and the Philippines. Duke, however, was killed in a crash at Dobodura, New Guinea, on June 18, 1943.

Joseph W. Stilwell (1883–1946)

Raised under a strict religious regimen that only brought out a rebellious side, Joseph Warren Stilwell graduated 32nd out of a class of 124 from the US Military Academy in 1904, and in 1918 he earned the Distinguished Service Cross for helping plan the strategy at St. Mihiel as IV Corps intelligence officer. Fluent in Chinese after three interwar tours in China, Lieutenant General Stilwell was serving as chief of staff to Chiang Kai-shek and with Chinese forces at Shwebo in late April 1942, when he learned that British, Indian, Burmese, and Chinese forces were abandoning Burma. On May 1, Stilwell set out on foot with what remained of his command—80 people, later growing to 114—to reach Imphal, India, on May 20. He was subsequently promoted to general in charge of South East Asia Command.

Above: A B-25B makes a training run from Ellington Field, Texas, to Eglin Field, Florida, on March 10, 1942, in preparation for an audacious attack on the Japanese home islands. To achieve this, 16 B-25Bs took off from the carrier *Hornet* on April 18, 1942, and bombed Tokyo and five other cities. The materially modest but psychologically stunning attack hastened Japanese efforts to seek a decisive confrontation with the US Fleet—and sparked reprisals that killed 250,000 Chinese.

Opposite top: A lineup of Douglas C-47 transport planes, which were as ubiquitous in the Pacific as they were in the European theater of operations. Based on the proven DC-3 airliner, the reliable C-47 encountered its greatest challenge after the Japanese cut off the Burma Road in April 1942, to which the Allies responded by initiating the India-China Ferry in May. This airlift required the C-47s to fly above their prescribed altitudes through the treacherous mountain passes of the eastern Himalayas.

Opposite: Captain Jack Renney resorts to his oxygen mask as he flies over the Himalayas from Assam to Kunming. Besides the C-47, the principal aircraft flying "The Hump," as the transport pilots called it, were the Curtiss C-46 Commando, the Douglas C-54 Skymaster, the Consolidated C-87 "Liberator Express" and its fuel-carrying cousin, the C-109. Started by the Tenth Air Force, the Hump flights were ultimately organized by the Air Transport Command.

James H. Doolittle (1896–1993)

The architect of the Tokyo raid (commonly known as the Doolittle Raid), Lieutenant Colonel James Harold Doolittle poses beside a recruiting poster inspired by his Tokyo raid. Born in Alameda, California, Doolittle was an army flight instructor in World War I and won numerous air races in the interwar years, as well as perfecting the art of "blind" flight on instruments alone in 1929. After bombing Tokyo, landing in China, and making his way back to the United States, Doolittle was awarded the Medal of Honor and subsequently commanded the Twelfth, Fifteenth, and Eighth Air Forces. He retired as a lieutenant general, but received a fourth star in 1985.

Above: On May 3, 1942, the Japanese occupied Tulagi in the Solomon Islands and began building a seaplane base. On the following day, aircraft from the carrier *Yorktown* raided Tulagi and sank the destroyer *Kikutsuki*, shown after being raised by the US Navy 34th Construction Battalion months later. Over the next few days, a Japanese attempt to seize Port Moresby brought on the war's first direct carrier confrontation in the Coral Sea.

Above: Grumman F4F-3As of *Yorktown*'s squadron VF-5 were among the participants in the Battle of the Coral Sea, in which *Yorktown*'s and *Lexington*'s planes sank the light carrier *Shoho* and damaged the large carrier *Shokaku*, but planes from *Shokaku* and *Zuikaku* sank *Lexington*, the oiler *Neosho* and destroyer *Sims*, and damaged *Yorktown*. Although tactically defeated, the Americans had turned back the invasion threat to Port Moresby, and *Yorktown*'s damage was repaired in time for the next battle at Midway.

Opposite: American soldiers stationed in the Aleutians clean their weapons in the wake of Japanese attacks in the North Pacific. On June 3, 1942, light carriers *Junyo* and *Ryujo* raided Dutch Harbor, Alaska, and Japanese troops landed on the Aleutian islands of Attu and Kiska. The primary purpose of what the Japanese dubbed Operation AL, to divide US naval forces and divert some from Midway Island, failed because the Americans, who had broken the Japanese codes, already knew Midway was their primary target.

Left: Curtiss P-40Es of Captain John S. Chennault's 11th Fighter Squadron sport their own variation on his father's "Flying Tigers" on an Aleutians airfield in the summer of 1943. Operating from Umnak, the 11th was among the defenders when the Japanese struck at Dutch Harbor, claiming six victories but losing two P-40s to *Junyo*'s Zeros, resulting in the death of one of its pilots, Lieutenant John C. Cape Jr.

Above: A Consolidated PBY-5A Catalina amphibious patrol bomber reconnoiters a snowy Aleutian landscape in late 1942. A PBY-5A of VP-42 was shot down by three of *Ryujo*'s Zeros during the Dutch Harbor raid, but one of those fighters was disabled by ground fire soon afterward and when its pilot tried to force land on Akutan Island, the plane flipped onto its back in the marshy ground, breaking his neck. A PBY crewman of VP-41 subsequently spotted the Zero, which was recovered and flown to gauge its capabilities and weaknesses.

Right: Among the marines defending Midway on June 4, 1942, was Captain Marion Carl of Fighting Squadron 221 (VMF-221). Flying an F4F-4 Wildcat against the carrier-launched attack, Carl was credited with a Zero destroyed and two others damaged, but of VMF-221's nine Wildcats and 19 Brewster F2A-1 Buffalos, only 10 planes returned and only two were flyable. Later, flying over Guadalcanal and the Solomons, Carl raised his score to 18½.

Below: Grumman TBF-1 Avengers, which made their combat debut at Midway. Detached to the island from carrier *Hornet*, six Avengers of Torpedo Squadron 8 (VT-8) joined land-based bombers—including four torpedo-equipped Martin B-26 Marauders—in an attack on the Japanese carriers, only to be met by their fighter defense. Five of the Avengers and two Marauders were among the heavy American losses, without scoring a hit on any Japanese ships.

"Sight what appears to be ten enemy surface ships, in position bearing 010 degrees distance 240 miles (386km) from Midway course 150 degrees, speed over 20 knots."

—*Report from Aichi E13A1 floatplane from heavy cruiser* Tone *to Japanese Combined Fleet at 0728 hours, June 4, 1942—failing to mention the presence of aircraft carriers in the American force until an hour later.*

Left: As the Japanese prepared to launch another strike on Midway, they learned that American carriers were in the area and were switching from bombs to torpedoes when they were attacked by aircraft from the island and carriers *Enterprise*, *Yorktown*, and *Hornet*. Leading F4F-4s of *Yorktown*'s VF-3, Lieutenant Commander John S. Thach used a mutual support tactic he'd devised, called the "Thach Weave," against as many as 20 Zeros, accounting for three while losing only one man from his flight.

Opposite: Lieutenant David R. Beery, serving as an instructor at the Air Operational Training Command, Jacksonville, Florida, in 1943, had previously earned the Navy Cross flying SBD-3s from *Yorktown* up to the Battle of Midway. While defending Zeros were slaughtering American torpedo bombers on June 4, dive bombers from *Yorktown* and *Enterprise* scored fatal hits on *Akagi*, *Kaga*, and *Soryu*. *Hiryu* and *Yorktown* were sunk later, as were heavy cruiser *Mikuma* and destroyer *Hammann*.

Chapter 2
Turning Tide
The Allies take the initiative

Opposite: After a shore bombardment, a destroyer crewman adds to the score on his ship's gun director, now totaling a ship torpedoed and two fighters and two bombers splashed. On August 6–7, 1943, Commander Frederick Moosbrugger used improved radar to ambush and sink three Japanese destroyers without loss in Vella Gulf, and on November 25 Captain Arleigh Burke repeated the performance off Cape St. George—signaling the end of the Tokyo Express's supremacy in night fighting.

"In the first six to twelve months of a war with the United States and Great Britain I will run wild and win victory upon victory," Admiral Isoroku Yamamoto had warned Prime Minister Fumimaro Konoe on the eve of hostilities. "But then, if the war continues after that, I have no expectation of success."

Japan's stunning successes in the months following Pearl Harbor proved Yamamoto's prediction remarkably prescient. So did the battles of Coral Sea and Midway, which ended his "wild" run on the early side of his prediction. The initiative in the Pacific was now up in the air, with an open question as to who would recover it. That answer came on August 7, 1942, when US Marines landed on Guadalcanal and seized the airfield the Japanese had begun to establish there. The six-month land, air, and sea struggle for that island did more than determine the initiative in the Solomon Islands. In September, with their army just 19 miles (30km) away from Port Moresby, the Japanese on New Guinea were forced to relinquish assets toward the retaking of Guadalcanal, allowing the Australians to mount a counterattack that drove the enemy back up the Kokoda Trail to Buna-Gona by November.

In the year following their evacuation of Guadalcanal, the Japanese fell back upon a defensive strategy, using the outermost islands they had taken as a buffer zone in which their soldiers, supported by ships and warplanes staging from Truk and Rabaul, would wear down the Allied forces until their governments sued for peace. The Allies indeed found New Guinea and the Solomons a slow and agonizing slog, but they proved no less horrific for the Japanese, who lost tens of thousands of their best-trained soldiers, sailors, and airmen in the jungles and shark-infested waters of the South Pacific.

Right: A 40mm Bofors antiaircraft gun stands guard over ships and a Short Sunderland flying boat operating under contract to the Directorate of Air Transport, Allied Forces, Australia, in Port Moresby harbor on April 26, 1943. In July 1942, Japanese troops landed at Buna and Gona in northern Papua New Guinea, and then marched on Port Moresby across the Owen Stanley Mountains and along the Kokoda Track, while outnumbered Australian militia conducted a fighting retreat.

Below: Photographed from the carrier *Wasp*, an old flush-deck, four-stack destroyer, soon to be modified for minesweeping and fast transport, lies before the troop transport *President Jackson* and other US Navy ships in New Caledonia on August 4, 1942, in preparation for the marine landings on Guadalcanal and Tulagi. These Solomon Island invasions were the first American offensives of World War II.

Right: Marine Commandant Lieutenant General Thomas Holcomb shows President Franklin D. Roosevelt a Japanese flag taken by Lieutenant Colonel Evans Carlson's Second Marine Raider Battalion on Makin Atoll's Butaritari Island in the Gilberts on August 17–18, 1942. Killing about 160 Japanese at a cost of 21 marines killed, two missing, and nine captured—the latter of whom were subsequently beheaded—the raid failed in its primary mission of diverting Japanese resources from Guadalcanal.

Below: Heavy cruiser *Chicago*, photographed from destroyer *Ellet*, supports the marines on Tulagi. Landing on August 7, the marines secured that and the adjacent isles of Gavutu and Tanambogo by the ninth. Off Savo Island that night, however, a Japanese cruiser force surprised and sank heavy cruisers USS *Astoria, Quincy*, and *Vincennes*, and HMAS *Canberra*, and damaged *Chicago*. The Allied fleet withdrew, leaving the marines on Guadalcanal to fend for themselves for weeks.

August 19–20, 1942 *British and Canadian troops raid Dieppe but are repulsed with heavy losses, while the Royal Air Force likewise takes a beating in the air.*

October–November 1942 *General Bernard Montgomery drives Rommel back in the Second Battle of El Alamein, while American and British forces land in Morocco and Algeria, forcing Axis forces to make a stand in Tunisia.*

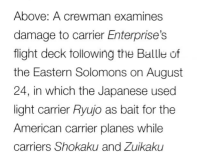

Above: A crewman examines damage to carrier *Enterprise*'s flight deck following the Battle of the Eastern Solomons on August 24, in which the Japanese used light carrier *Ryujo* as bait for the American carrier planes while carriers *Shokaku* and *Zuikaku* destroyed *Enterprise*, *Wasp*, and *Saratoga*. *Ryujo* was indeed sunk, but the three bombs that struck *Enterprise* did not eliminate it. The new antiaircraft light cruiser *Atlanta*, in the background, contributed to the carriers' defense.

Opposite: Boeing B-17E Flying Fortress bombers take off from Henderson Field. Concurrent with the Battle of the Eastern Solomons on August 24 was an attack on a Japanese convoy of reinforcements to Guadalcanal by Henderson-based SBDs, which sank the transport *Kinryu Maru*. When destroyer *Mutsuki* came to the ship's aid and B-17s also attacked, the Japanese captain contemptuously ignored the bombers—and paid dearly when one 500-pound (227kg) bomb hit and sank his ship.

November–December 1942 *In spite of massive casualties, Soviet forces stop the Germans at Stalingrad and in the Caucasus Mountains, and then counterattack, encircling the German Sixth Army in Stalingrad.*

February 19–25, 1943 *Field Marshal Erwin Rommel strikes back at the advancing US Army in Tunisia, inflicting a humiliating defeat on it at Kasserine Pass, but is forced to withdraw due to overstretched logistics.*

Left: *Saratoga*—seen here at Pearl Harbor's Ford Island prior to deployment—launched 38 planes in response to *Ryujo*'s raid on Guadalcanal's recently seized airstrip, named Henderson Field by the Americans. *Saratoga* caught the light carrier while most of its own aircraft were engaged in their attack, sinking *Ryujo* and damaging seaplane carrier *Chitose*. On August 31, however, a torpedo from submarine *I-26* forced *Saratoga* to leave the Solomons for major repairs.

The WAVE Contribution

As the US Navy's commitment to two major fronts grew, August 1942 saw the formation of Women Accepted for Volunteer Emergency Service. The WAVES' first commander, Lieutenant Commander Mildred McAfee, had been president of Wellesley College before receiving the first female officer's commission in US Navy history. By the end of 1942, 27,000 women were performing a growing variety of noncombat tasks, freeing up more men to serve overseas.

Although their name implied a strictly war emergency role, the WAVES differed from the Women's Auxiliary Army Corps in that they were an integral part of the navy, getting equal pay for their ranks and subject to the same discipline as their male colleagues. The army would later similarly incorporate its female personnel as the Women's Army Corps, or WACs. The WAVES did not accept black women until 1944, one out of 36 WAVES being black by the end of the war. On June 12, 1948, the Women's Armed Services Integration Act officially made women a part of the armed forces, and the WAVES officially ceased to exist.

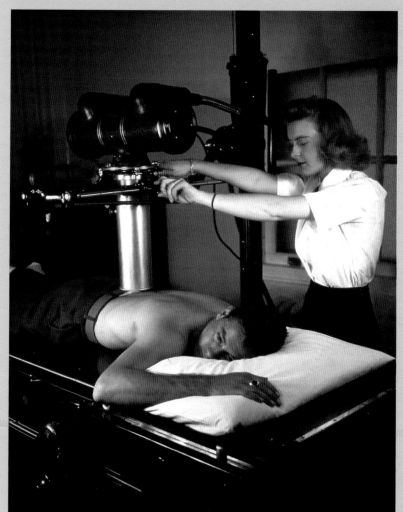

Above: Mailman First Class Della Marie Stout sorts airmail letters bound for overseas units at the Fleet Post Office in San Francisco, California.

Left: Aerographer's Mate Second Class Julia Murray launches a weather balloon to check the rate of wind velocity at NAS Santa Ana, California.

Opposite top: Specialist Second Class (Photographic) Martha Louis McClelland, a scriptwriter at the Training Films Division, makes notes as a diver descends to perform before underwater cameras.

Opposite left: Aviation mechanics Lorraine Taylor (atop nacelle) and Martha Harrison work on the number one engine of a Douglas R5D Skymaster of Transport Squadron 4 (VR-4) at Naval Air Station Oakland, California.

Opposite right: Winifred Peroksy, a WAVE at the US Naval Hospital in San Diego, California, x-rays Marine Private First Class Harold E. Reyher, who had been wounded by a sniper on Iwo Jima in February 1945.

Left: Mailman Second Class Violet Louella Buxman checks V-mail for legibility through a film viewer at FPO San Francisco. Microfilming brief V-mail letters allowed a vastly greater volume to be transported quickly to and from the war zones, providing an invaluable boost to morale, both military and civilian.

Above: Army soldiers guard the coast near Astoria, Oregon, in October 1942. On September 9 and 29, 1942, a Yokosuka E14Y1 floatplane from the submarine *I-25* dropped incendiary bombs in an Oregon forest—the first aerial bombing of the US mainland. Previous days of rainy weather prevented the fires from spreading, but the incident did increase alarm along the northwest coast.

Opposite: Responding to Japanese submarine activity with similar prudence to their American allies, Canadian volunteer rangers patrol their Pacific coast in October 1942. A squadron of Canadian Curtiss P-40Es would later serve in the Aleutians, and 5,300 Canadians would take part in the Kiska landings in August 1943.

"Our food is completely gone. We are eating tree bark and grass . . . In other units there are men eating the flesh of dead Australians."

—*A Japanese machine gunner of the 144th Infantry Regiment writing in his diary of his unit's retreat through the Owen Stanley Mountains of New Guinea, late summer 1942.*

Above: An American soldier in the Andreanof Islands scans the horizon for Japanese aircraft in 1942. The Japanese occupation of Attu and Kiska led to the Americans establishing bases on several Aleutian Islands as well. Intermittent air raids were exchanged as weather permitted, and Japanese attempts to keep their garrisons supplied were attended by the loss of several ships and submarines.

Above: In spite of resistance from Australian troops like this one, the Japanese advanced to within 20 miles (32km) of Port Moresby by September 1942. At that point, however, with their supply lines overstretched and their high command concerned with Guadalcanal and the threat of an American move on Buna, they were ordered to withdraw. Their retreat, begun on the twenty-eighth, was pursued by the Australians all the way back to Buna-Gona.

"We had no control tower, just a radio and an operations tent. We had no runway boundary lights and no revetments. If someone came in late, jeeps would set up a couple of lights down the field, so we could see it at night."

—John B. Maas, Marine Fighter Squadron VMF-112, on Henderson Field.

Opposite: Soldiers of the 32nd Infantry Division undergo amphibious training at Camp Cable, Queensland, in the summer of 1942. On October 14, the division began advancing on the Australian right flank along the Kapa Kapa Trail, and on November 16 the Allied forces attacked Buna and Gona. Gona fell on December 9, Buna on January 2, 1943, Sanananda on the twelfth, and the last Japanese survivors escaped north on the twenty-second. By then the 32nd Division had lost 586 men killed in combat, 100 dead of other causes, 1,954 wounded, and 7,125 suffering from disease, of whom 2,952 required hospitalization.

"In New Guinea, it rains every day for nine months, and then the rainy season begins."

—An Australian officer to newly arrived American Lieutenant Robert H. Odell, 126th Regiment, 32nd Infantry Division, October 1942.

Above: While the marines on Guadalcanal fought off a succession of Japanese army assaults, marine Grumman F4F-4 Wildcats—sometimes supplemented by their navy colleagues, who sometimes rotated on and off the carriers, and by army planes of the Thirteenth Air Force—defended Henderson Field against Japanese aircraft and bombarding warships. Five marine Wildcat aces, Harold W. Bauer, Joseph J. Foss, Robert E. Galer, Jefferson DeBlanc, and John L. Smith, were awarded the Medal of Honor in the course of the campaign.

William F. Halsey Jr. (1882–1959)

Born in Elizabeth, New Jersey, the son of a US Navy captain, William Frederick Halsey Jr. excelled more in sports than academics at the Naval Academy. Serving mostly aboard destroyers before getting a carrier command instilled an aggressive, if not always prudent, attitude that became his trademark. On October 18, 1942, Admiral Nimitz replaced the pessimistic Vice Admiral Robert L. Ghormley with Vice Admiral Halsey as commander of the US Navy in the Southwest Pacific. "I had to begin throwing punches almost immediately," Halsey reported to Nimitz, as the Japanese precipitated another attempt at a decisive naval battle off the Santa Cruz Islands on October 26.

Below: A PBY-5A pilot from a night-flying "Black Cat" squadron reads mail from home at a South Pacific base. The first aggressive use of the Catalina occurred off Guadalcanal on October 15, 1942, when Major Jack R. Cram, pilot of Major General Roy S. Geiger's PBY-5A *Blue Goose*, attacked a Japanese convoy with two torpedoes, sinking the transport *Sasago Maru*. After *Blue Goose* returned with 175 bullet holes, Geiger dressed down Cram for jeopardizing government property . . . then recommended him for the Navy Cross.

Above: Crewmen perform maintenance on a Grumman TBF-1. The Battle of Santa Cruz, fought on October 26, 1942, began with both sides attacking each other simultaneously.

Spotting some Avengers from *Enterprise*'s Torpedo Squadron VT-10, Lieutenant Saneyasu Hidaka of light carrier *Zuiho*'s fighter group peeled off after the Americans. Hidaka's nine

Zeros downed two TBFs and damaged two others along with three F4Fs but lost four pilots, and he was criticized after the war for abandoning his escort mission.

Below: SBD-3s follow an F4F-4 into takeoff position aboard a US Navy carrier in 1942. The Battle of Santa Cruz ended with the carrier *Hornet* and destroyer *Smith* sunk, plus *Enterprise* damaged, but the serious damage the Americans inflicted on carriers *Shokaku* and *Zuiho*, combined with heavy Japanese aircrew losses—148 compared to 26 Americans—prevented the Japanese fleet from following up on its pyrrhic tactical victory.

Left: Troop transport *Yamazuki Maru* was one of four run aground near Tassafaronga Point by Rear Admiral Raizo Tanaka on November 15, 1943, after losing seven other ships to American air attacks. "Tenacious" Tanaka's decision got 2,000 soldiers, 260 cases of ammunition, and 1,500 bags of rice ashore, but the Japanese lost battleships *Hiei* and *Kirishima* during the naval battles of November 13–15—and ultimately the initiative at Guadalcanal.

Above: Heavy cruiser *Minneapolis* departs Pearl Harbor on April 11, 1943, after repairs to its bow, which was blown off during the Battle of Tassafaronga. There, on November 29, 1942, an American cruiser force ambushed Raizo Tanaka's "Tokyo Express" and sank destroyer *Takanami*, but his destroyer torpedoes sank heavy cruiser *Northampton* and damaged *Pensacola*, *New Orleans*, and *Minneapolis*. Tanaka failed to deliver most of his cargo, however, and by then the Guadalcanal campaign's outcome had been decided.

Raizo Tanaka (1892–1969)

Born in Yamaguchi City, Raizo Tanaka graduated 34th out of 118 in the Imperial Naval Academy's class of 1913. He became a specialist in the use of Japan's Type 93 "Long Lance" torpedo when he took command of Destroyer Squadron 2 in September 1941. Flying his pennant from light cruiser *Jintsu*, Rear Admiral Tanaka led his destroyers through the Philippine campaign, the Battle of the Java Sea on February 27, 1942, and escorted the troops transports for the landing at Midway that never occurred. His greatest fame, however, came in leading the transport runs to Guadalcanal that the Americans called the "Tokyo Express." Tanaka's outspokenness later got him reassigned to shore duty, although he was promoted to vice admiral in October 1944, and retired from the navy in 1946.

> "I have heard that the US Naval experts praised my command in that action. I am not deserving of such honors. It was the superb proficiency and devotion of the men who served me that produced the tactical victory for us."

—Rear Admiral Raizo Tanaka, commander of Japanese Destroyer Squadron 2, a.k.a. the "Tokyo Express," on the Battle of Tassafaronga, November 29, 1942.

Opposite: The pilot and chief engineer of a Consolidated PB4Y-1 Privateer look at maps of New Georgia before departing Henderson Field on a bombing run against the Japanese air base there in December 1942. The navy version of the B-24D Liberator, the PB4Y-1 joined its Thirteenth Air Force cousins in strikes on Japanese sea and air bases throughout the Solomon Island chain up to their main base at Rabaul, New Britain, frequently running a gauntlet of Zeros, with or without fighter escort of its own.

Joseph J. Foss (1915–2003)

Born in Sioux Falls, South Dakota, Joseph Jacob Foss worked on his father's farm until 1940, when he joined the Marine Corps. Flying F4F-4 Wildcats from Henderson Field as fighter squadron VMF-121's executive officer, Captain Foss downed a Zero in his first fight—and survived being shot down himself—on October 13, 1942. Three Zeros shot down on January 15, 1943, brought his tally to 26—the marine record—and that of his eight-plane flight, known as "Joe's Flying Circus," to 61.5. Awarded the Medal of Honor, he retired a brigadier general, also serving in South Dakota's state legislature and, from 1955 to 1959, as its governor.

"Total and complete defeat of Japanese forces on Guadalcanal effected today. Tokyo Express no longer has terminus on Guadalcanal."

—*Major General Alexander M. Patch, commander, 23rd "Americal" Infantry Division, February 9, 1943.*

Left: US Army troops carry supplies from an LCM (landing craft, mechanized) on Guadalcanal in January 1943. On October 24, the 23rd Infantry Division (dubbed "Americal" in reference to New Caledonia, where it was formed) helped repulse a Japanese attack on Henderson Field and took the offensive on November 5. Relieving the exhausted 1st Marine Division in December, the Americal, together with the 25th Infantry and 2nd Marine Divisions, completed the conquest on Guadalcanal on February 9, 1943.

Above: C-47s of the 6th Carrier Squadron, Fifth Air Force, flying from Wards Drome, Port Moresby, carry supplies to the Australian "Kanga Force" at Wau. On January 29, 1943, the Japanese 102nd Regiment, led by Major General Tooru Okabe, moved on Wau to preempt Australian plans to attack their beachheads at Lae and Salamaua. Reinforced by Brigadier Murray Moten's 17th Brigade, Kanga Force repulsed the assault by the thirty-first, suffering 349 casualties but killing some 1,200 Japanese.

Right: Australian soldiers at Wau unload cargo from a C-47 of the 6th Carrier Squadron on April 27, 1943. After defending Wau, the ad hoc Kanga Force, which had been harassing the Japanese since April 1942, was disbanded and, with the 17th Brigade, incorporated into the 3rd Division. On April 22 the 3rd Division, commanded by Major General Stanley G. Savige, marched out of Wau to retake Lae and Salamaua.

Above: A Consolidated PB2Y-3R Coronado flying boat loads cargo at the Pan Am Airways dock at Treasure Island, California, in January 1943, with the San Francisco Bay Bridge and Yerba Buena Island in the background. Having less than half the range of the PBY patrol bomber, Coronados were used as aerial freighters by the Naval Air Transport Service. The PB4Y-3R, of which 31 were built, had a side loading hatch and accommodations for 44 people.

Left: A gunner trains in an SNJ at Naval Air Station Miami, Florida, on April 9, 1943. A stepped-up training program replaced American losses faster than the Japanese could theirs. During Operation I, a Japanese air onslaught in the Solomons and New Guinea in April 1943, Lockheed P-38s of the 339th Fighter Squadron intercepted and downed two G4M1 bomber-transports over Bougainville on April 18. One of the passengers killed was truly irreplaceable for the Japanese: Admiral Isoroku Yamamoto.

The Vought Corsair

The first American fighter capable of 400mph (644kph), the Vought F4U-1 Corsair was rejected by the navy as unsuitable for carrier takeoff and landings, and passed on to the marines—who, after a rough combat debut on February 14, 1943, soon adapted their tactics to the plane's strengths by avoiding low-speed dogfights with their Japanese counterparts in favor of hit-and-run attacks or head-on confrontations that made the most of their superior speed, firepower, and ability to take punishment. By May 1943, the marine Corsair units had taken the Zero's measure and universally concluded that, for once, their navy castoff was a winner.

Among the first aces in the F4U, Kenneth Walsh of VMF-124 developed its early tactical doctrine, and his 22 victories, including four on August 30, 1943, earned him the Medal of Honor. Robert M. Hanson of VMF-215 scored 25 before being killed in action on February 4, 1944, receiving a posthumous Medal of Honor. Gregory Boyington, leader of VMF-214, added 22 enemy planes to the two he'd downed earlier with the American Volunteer Group in China. Although shot down on January 3, 1944, "Pappy" Boyington survived that and enemy captivity to receive his "posthumous" Medal of Honor from President Harry Truman after the war.

Below: Vought F4U-1 Corsairs line up for a mission from Fighter 2 airfield on Guadalcanal in the spring of 1943.

Right: A Corsair taxies along a South Pacific runway in 1943. Besides the marines, Navy Squadron VF-17, the "Jolly Rogers," produced several F4U aces, including Lieutenant Ira C. Kepford with 16 victories.

> "I think every Marine who flew it would agree that one of the nicest things the Navy did for us during the war was to give us the Corsair."
>
> —John B. Maas, Marine Fighter Squadron VMF-112, on the Vought F4U-1.

Above: First Lieutenant Robert W. McClurg, shown in May 1944 after his Solomons tour, became a "Black Sheep" ace under "Pappy" Boyington's tutelage in VMF-214, downing seven Japanese aircraft.

Opposite: Featuring a bubble canopy and other improvements, an F4U-1A of Gregory Boyington's "Black Sheep" Squadron VMF-214 prepares to depart Vella Lavella in late 1943. VMF-214 claimed 94 enemy planes for the loss of 12 pilots.

"I had only 21 hours of training in fighters before I was sent to the Pacific. Most pilots had experienced 125–200 hours. When Pappy first saw me fly, he said, 'Kid, you'll never make it home unless I teach you something.' He did just that and I became one of Pappy's wingmen."

—Bob McClurg, VMF-214.

Above: Aviation Ordnanceman N. F. Nitishin carries belts of .50-caliber ammunition to feed the six machine guns on a Corsair at a Pacific air base. The bullets are arranged in a mix of one red-nosed tracer to four armor-piercing rounds. Japanese Solomons ace Tetsuzo Iwamoto commented that one could tell a downed plane's nationality by the debris in the water: If the wreckage was floating, it was American; if it was burning on the water, it was most likely Japanese.

George C. Kenney (1879–1977)

Born in Nova Scotia, Canada, but educated in Brookline, Massachusetts, George Churchill Kenney flew 75 missions and scored two aerial victories in Salmson 2A2s with the 91st Aero Squadron in World War I. In August 1942 he took charge of General MacArthur's air assets in the Southwest Pacific, and between March 2 and 4, 1943, his Fifth Air Force, with the Royal Australian Air Force, wiped out a New Guinea-bound troop convoy in the Battle of the Bismarck Sea. By April 1944, the Fifth Air Force had annihilated the Japanese Fourth Air Army in New Guinea, and later that year Lieutenant General Kenney commanded the Far East Air Force, encompassing the Fifth, Seventh, and Thirteenth Air Forces.

Left: A Mitsubishi A6M3 Zero, either forced to land after being shot-up in an aerial engagement, or caught in an American air strike, lies out of commission on Munda, New Georgia. Attaining its formidable combination of speed, climb, maneuverability, heavy armament, and phenomenal range, largely by means of lightweight construction with no armor or self-sealing fuel tanks, the Zero could not keep pace with second-generation American fighters, such as the F4U Corsair or P-38 Lightning.

Below: A typical component of Kenney's Fifth Air Force, B-25C-1 41-21971 started with the 38th Bomb Group in September 1942, participating in the Battle of the Bismarck Sea. It later transferred to the 500th Squadron of the 345th Bomb Group, piloted by First Lieutenant Victor Tatelman, and was decorated with the squadron's "Bats Outa Hell" nose marking in December 1943. When retired as "war weary" in August 1944, Dirty Dora had flown 175 bombing and strafing missions.

"If the son of a bitch wants to fight, I'll give him a fight!"

—Lieutenant Commander Andrew J. Hill, captain of destroyer Nicholas, *regarding a Japanese destroyer spotted during the night Battle of Kula Gulf, July 6, 1943.* Mochizuki, *an obsolescent troop-carrying destroyer, did not actually want a fight, launching a torpedo that missed the pursuing destroyers* Nicholas *and* Radford, *and after taking two shell hits laid smoke and escaped.*

Left: The nocturnal bombardment of Munda and Vila by Task Force 18 on May 13, 1943, silhouettes the number three 5-inch (12.5cm) gun turret aboard destroyer *Nicholas* (DD-449). An early example of the prolific, versatile *Fletcher* class, *Nicholas* took part in numerous night battles with Japanese destroyer convoys into the Solomons that the Americans called the "Tokyo Express," including Kula Gulf (5–6 July) and Kolombangara (12–13 July).

Above: An air controller in the Southwest Pacific Area radios a returning airplane and records its flight information while his partners scan the sky for more planes. Most control towers in New Guinea and the Solomons were open on all sides, exposing their personnel to the elements. Once they took up station in the tower, the air controllers were not authorized to leave it until all aircraft had landed or were accounted for.

February–March 1943 *Field Marshal Friedrich Paulus surrenders the last of the Sixth Army in Stalingrad, but Field Marshal Erich von Manstein manages to defeat the Soviet follow-up offensive and retakes Kharkov.*

March 1943 *Major General George S. Patton Jr. wins his first victory over the Germans at El Guettar, and General Bernard Law Montgomery inflicts a costly defeat on Rommel at Medenine.*

Below: A Kawasaki Ki.48 of the 45th *Koku Sentai* (air regiment), found abandoned when the marines captured Munda airfield on August 5, was shipped to Lunga Point, Guadalcanal, for evaluation and eventual scrapping. Code-named "Lily" by the Allies, the Ki.48 was a twin-engine light bomber used by the Japanese army throughout the war in China and the Pacific, though its performance proved disappointing and its defensive armament inadequate.

Left: The crew of a camouflaged Higgins-type PT (patrol torpedo) boat trains for operations in the Solomons. With wooden hulls 78 feet long (24m) for the Higgins and 80 feet (25m) for the Elco-built variants, PT boats performed a variety of tasks, usually under the cover of night, such as scouting and intelligence gathering, rescuing downed airmen, dropping or picking up coast watchers, ambushing enemy supply convoys, or shooting up coastal installations.

May 1943 *Axis forces in Tunisia surrender to Allies, who take 230,000 prisoners. After losing 27 U-boats between mid-April and end of May, Admiral Karl Dönitz withdraws wolf packs, marking a turning point in the Battle of the Atlantic.*

July 1943 *Germany's last bid to seize the initiative in the Soviet Union fails in the Battle of Kursk, while British and American forces land in Sicily. RAF bombing of Hamburg on July 30 creates a firestorm that kills 42,600 civilians.*

Right: Captain A. P. Calvert of the Bureau of Ships' PT Boat Design Section describes a Higgins boat's features to Lieutenant Commander E. B. Coulter of the PT Boat Maintenance Section, in a room decorated with PT squadron emblems. Calvert had led Motor Torpedo Boat Flotilla 1 in the South Pacific. A future president, Lieutenant John F. Kennedy commanded Elco boat PT-109 until it was rammed and sunk by Japanese destroyer *Amagiri* on the night of August 1–2, 1943.

Above: A signalman aboard the *Crater*-class cargo ship *Sculptor* (AK-103) communicates with another vessel in a convoy carrying Lend-Lease equipment to New Zealand on October 5, 1943. The Japanese failure to use their submarines against Allied merchant shipping to the extent that the Germans did in the Atlantic—and, for that matter, the Americans did against Japanese shipping—was a major factor in their ultimate defeat.

Northern Sideshow

Neither the Japanese nor the Americans had much desire to fight in the Aleutian Islands, which the latter called "Birthplace of Bad Weather." In June 1942, however, the Japanese attacked Dutch Harbor, Alaska, and landed on Attu and Kiska, hoping to divert a portion of the US Navy from their actual objective, Midway. The feint failed, leaving the Japanese in possession of two desolate specks of American soil, and the United States determined to take it back.

The next year saw air and sea actions, including an inconclusive cruiser battle off the Komandorski islands on March 27, 1943, before the Americans landed on Attu on May 11, 1943. The defenders withdrew inland and the Americans suffered 898 dead, 1,148 injured, 1,200 frostbitten, and 614 cases of disease, before the Japanese expended their last lives in a banzai charge near Massacre Bay on May 29, their losses totaling 2,351 dead and only 28 captured.

On August 15, 1943, 19,126 American and 5,300 Canadian troops landed on Kiska, suffering 313 casualties to booby traps and friendly fire incidents. There were no Japanese—a cruiser and destroyer force had evacuated the entire garrison under the Allies' noses on July 28. For the rest of the war, the American Eleventh Air Force and US Navy bombed the Japanese northern naval base at Paramushir, flying 1,500 sorties. Material damage was modest, but it diverted some 500 Japanese aircraft and 41,000 soldiers to guard their northern approaches instead of seeing more vitally needed service elsewhere.

Above: Sergeant Clark E. Hilliard carries metal-link ammunition to reload the .50-caliber guns of a North American B-25 of the Eleventh Air Force in Alaska in 1943. Note the radar array under the bombardier's position.

Left: American soldiers come ashore on an Aleutians beachhead. Although the Allies had every reason to expect trouble, the bloody fight for Attu took place further inland, and the Americans and Canadians landing at Kiska encountered no Japanese at all.

Opposite: Four Eleventh Air Force pilots discuss their next mission just before takeoff.

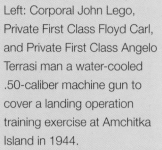

Left: Corporal John Lego, Private First Class Floyd Carl, and Private First Class Angelo Terrasi man a water-cooled .50-caliber machine gun to cover a landing operation training exercise at Amchitka Island in 1944.

Below: After an Eleventh Air Force photoreconnaissance sortie, Captain Nils Peterson transfers data from an annotated photograph, showing construction and destruction to Japanese facilities in the Kurile Islands, to maps and charts.

Left: Lieutenant General George C. Kenney speaks to mechanics, (from left) Staff Sergeant Clyde Sims, Tech Sergeant James Freeman, and Tech Sergeant Victor Cunningham, at an Australian air base on October 28, 1943. By that time, fighters, attack planes, and medium bombers of Kenney's Fifth Air Force were regularly attacking Japanese air bases throughout New Guinea, and his heavy bombers were striking regularly as far up the Solomons as Rabaul.

Below left: An airman of the 345th Bomb Group poses proudly under his unit's emblem, which was applied to the vertical stabilizers of its B-25s. With their noses packed with up to eight .50-caliber machine guns or cannons ranging from 20 to 75 millimeters, the "Air Apaches" specialized in skip-bombing ships and strafing airfields, also employing "parafrag" bombs with small parachutes to slow their descent and allow the low-flying bombers to get clear before they exploded.

Opposite: Guadalcanal had been reduced to a staging area when it suffered its last great disaster on November 26, 1943, and ironically the enemy played no part in it. Instead, a fire broke out in the ammunition dump on Hell's Point and touched off a chain reaction of exploding bullets, shells, rockets, flamethrowers, and fuel that spread to Henderson Field. Two soldiers and 15 patients in a nearby hospital were killed in the conflagration and series of blasts, which continued for three days.

"Hello DS 23. Hang onto your hats boys, here we go."

—*Captain Arleigh A. Burke to officers of Destroyer Squadron 23 before attacking five Japanese destroyers off Cape St. George on the night of November 25, 1943, sinking three without loss.*

"... one of the gangster leaders in a gangster group in a gangster-ridden country."

—*Tokyo Rose, referring to Lieutenant General George Kenney, after a devastating low-level air strike on the Japanese air base at Nadzab, New Guinea, by Fifth Air Force B-25s, on March 23, 1943.*

Chapter 3

Island Hopping

Breaking Japan's defensive outer ring

Opposite: A marine, wearing a tattoo to "Lorene," avails himself of his canteen as he peers out of a seriously perforated Japanese steel bunker on one of Kwajalein's islets. Devastating as the bombardment had been, the most telling demonstration of lessons learned from Tarawa was the continuous support that the ships and carrier planes provided the troops until the atoll was secured on February 3, 1944.

The late summer of 1943 and early 1944 saw the start of two manifestations of what came to be called the "island hopping" strategy, widely attributed to both General Douglas MacArthur and Admiral Chester W. Nimitz. In the former's case, it involved the US and Australian armies bypassing the bulk of the Japanese army in New Guinea to secure a series of key points along its northern coast, followed by the island of Morotai and the Palau Islands before moving on MacArthur's main target, the Philippines. Meanwhile, Nimitz unleashed a resurgent US Navy into the Central Pacific, seizing key islands, neutralizing dangerous staging bases, such as Truk, and bypassing the rest, leaving their cut-off garrisons to fend for themselves.

The first actions quickly established the supremacy of the new generation of US Navy carrier planes, most dramatically the Grumman F6F-3 Hellcat fighter, which swiftly got the better of the latest models of Mitsubishi A6M Zero. Even with virtual air superiority, however, the Americans did not always have things their own way. For one thing, the Japanese seemed to employ a different defensive strategy on each island group they held, with equally diverse results—sometimes swiftly succumbing to overwhelming firepower, but sometimes using well-prepared defenses in-depth to inflict heavy attrition on the invaders. For another, no matter how great the US Fleet's predominance, the odd airplane or submarine, guided by determined crews, could still occasionally slip in to rouse the Americans from any sense of complacency by inflicting a bitter loss.

Chester W. Nimitz (1885–1966)

Born in Fredericksburg, Texas, Chester William Nimitz was unable to get an appointment to the US Military Academy, instead entering the Naval Academy, from which he graduated seventh in 1905's class of 114. As commander in chief of the Pacific Fleet (CinCPac), Admiral Nimitz formulated a plan to close in on Japan by a more direct route than his army colleague, General Douglas MacArthur, had in mind in the South Pacific. This would involve using a new, expanding carrier force to seize a string of island bases across the Central Pacific, starting with the Gilberts and Marshalls, neutralizing and bypassing other Japanese strongholds along the way.

Opposite top left: US Navy veterans in dress blue uniforms, all sporting aircrewmen's badges over their campaign ribbons, pose confidently under the wing of a Grumman TBF-1C Avenger. By 1943, the navy had grown in both the number of ships and the personnel to crew them, and the latter profited from the experience of instructors who had survived the critical sea and air battles of 1942.

Opposite top right: All eyes turn skyward to *Yorktown*'s port side during an air defense exercise, with antiaircraft (AA) gun positions manned and ready. Japanese aircraft had taken their toll against three of the four fleet carriers lost by the US Navy in 1942, and consequently the *Essex*-class's AA armament had been considerably strengthened, including twelve 5-inch (12.5cm) dual-purpose guns firing ammunition with VT ("variable time") fuzes, which were actually radio activated to explode upon detecting targets within 70 feet (21.5m).

Opposite left: The crewman of one of *Yorktown*'s 17 quadruple Bofors gun positions, in this case on the control tower or "island," feeds 40mm rounds into the magazine during an exercise. He wears a protective antiflash mask, steel helmet, and life jacket. In addition to the 40mm guns, each *Essex*-class carrier carried 65 20mm Oerlikon guns, which in concert with the 5-inchers (12.5cm) laid a formidable barrage.

Opposite right: Named for her predecessor sunk at Midway, the second USS *Yorktown* (CV-10) was the second of 24 *Essex*-class fleet carriers that would be built in the course of the war. Unencumbered by the voided restrictions of the Washington Treaty, *Essex* (CV-9) and her sisters were 872 feet long (266m), 93 feet (28.5m) in beam, and could carry 90 to 100 *planes—Lexington* (CV-16), at one point, carried 110—at speeds of up to 33 knots.

Right: First flying in June 1942 and entering combat with land-based units in the Solomons in September 1943, the Grumman F6F-3 Hellcat incorporated improvements by codesigners Leroy R. Grumman and William T. Schwendler to their earlier F4F Wildcat. The Hellcat had the largest wing area on a single-engine American fighter and a loaded weight of six tons (5.5 tonnes), but its 2,000hp Pratt & Whitney R-2800-10 Double Wasp radial engine gave it a maximum speed of 375mph (603kph) and maneuverability comparable to the Zero's.

Left: An F6F-3 pilot awaits the takeoff signal aboard *Yorktown*, in a photograph by Lieutenant Commander Charles Kerlee. Concurrent with the carrier air groups, Hellcats entered combat with squadrons VF-33 and VF-38 in the Solomons in August 1943, and by September had established their superiority over the A6M3 Zeros they encountered in that area of operations. The carrier-based Hellcats would not get their chance against Zeros until October.

Opposite: Gunner of a Douglas SBD-5 aims twin .30-caliber machine guns during *Independence*'s shakedown cruise. Built on the hulls of *Cleveland*-class light cruisers, the 11,000-ton (9,979 tonnes) *Independence*-class light carriers were 622 feet 6 inches long (190m), had a flight deck width of 109 feet 2 inches (33m), and steamed at up to 31.5 knots. Usually carrying 24 fighters and nine torpedo planes, they supplemented the *Essex*-class ships in each task group.

August 1, 1943 *In the first of many massed attacks on the Romanian oil refineries at Ploesti, 163 Consolidated B-24 Liberators bomb the facilities at low altitude, but 41 are shot down, five lost to other causes, and eight interned in Turkey.*

August 17, 1943 *The US Eighth Air Force bombs factories at Schweinfurt and Regensburg, but loses 60 of the 376 participating Boeing B-17s as well as five fighters, showing the critical need for long-range fighter escorts.*

September 3–16, 1943 *American and British forces land at Salerno, amid which Italy capitulates to the Allies on September 8, although the Germans rescue the imprisoned Benito Mussolini and establish a Fascist Italian rump state in the north.*

November 6, 1943 *Climaxing their campaign to liberate the Ukraine, Soviet forces secure Kiev, but German counterattacks continue around the city with mutually heavy losses until both sides fall into exhausted stalemate on December 22.*

Left: An aviation ordnanceman checks the ammunition feed to the twin .30-caliber machine guns in the rear cockpit of an SBD-5 in the hangar of an escort carrier. The pink cap with black stripe identifies his job on the flight deck. Besides their primary mission of protecting convoys from submarines, the relatively slow and lightly constructed escort carriers on both sides were often tasked with ferrying aircraft to island bases.

Above: An aviation machinist's mate works on the pitch control of a three-bladed propeller. No less important than the airmen's training was that of the maintenance crews, who for every hour of combat flying had to spend several times as much repairing and checking each plane upon its return to make sure that it would be fit for the next mission.

Training the Fleet

As important as the exponential growth of American weapons production was the concurrent increase in training. While Japan expended a high proportion of its best trained and experienced seamen and aircrews in the Solomons and New Guinea, the United States rotated its veteran survivors of the early campaigns to share their experience with their successors-to-be, and made a regular practice of doing so with each new generation of fighting personnel. The result manifested itself not only in overwhelming numbers of ships and planes, but in the consistency of the men who operated them.

"I got through primary training at Livermore, Calif., in two months, then went to Corpus Christi, Texas, for advanced training," recalled John Theodore Crosby. "I got my wings and was commissioned an ensign on May 15, 1943. I then went to Miami, Fla., for field carrier practice and to the Great Lakes to qualify on the training carrier *Wolverine*, a converted coal carrier, often taking off and landing in a North American SNJ with a 30-knot wind across the deck."

Ted Crosby went on to fly F6F-3s in squadron VF-18 aboard carrier *Bunker Hill*. Later, flying F6F-5s with VF-17 from *Hornet*, he shot down five kamikazes within an hour on April 16, 1945.

Above: "Spoiler, the original Flight Deck Dope," demonstrates what *not* to do aboard the escort carrier: cap unbuckled, no life belt while the ship is underway, leaning on the propeller of a Douglas SBD with his mind on anything but his job.

Left: The refueling crew aboard an escort carrier, engaged in training exercises in 1943, gasses up a Grumman TBF-1, with a fire extinguisher operator at the ready.

Opposite: The training escort carrier's flight deck officer signals Fly Control on the bridge that the SBDs and TBFs on deck are checked out and ready for the next training flight.

Left: A catapult crew member (in green cap and jersey) and his talker (in white) train at the signal board that connects their catwalk position to the catapult machinery room.

Below: "Hot papas," Fire Rescue personnel in asbestos-lined suits, stand by at their amidships flight station on the escort carrier, ready for trouble during the deck landings.

Above: An arrestor gear crewman, whose role is indicated by his green cap and jersey, operates the wheel that raises and lowers the flight deck barrier during a deck operations exercise. Note yellow primer on the training ship's structure.

Left: A 40mm gun crew aboard *Yorktown* stands ready as the carrier, accompanied by two destroyers in the background, approaches its first target in the summer of 1943. The first strike, by Task Force 15.5, commanded by Rear Admiral Charles A. Pownall and centered on carriers *Essex, Yorktown*, and *Independence*, was Marcus Island, 1,568 miles (2,523km) from Midway and less than 1,000 miles (1,609km) from Tokyo.

Above: A Grumman TBF-1C Avenger, carrying bombs instead of a torpedo, takes off from *Yorktown*. When Task Force 15.5 attacked it on August 31, 1943, Marcus's garrison was caught by surprise. Six air strikes totaling 275 sorties destroyed several G4M2 "Betty" bombers on the airfield as well as various island installations. No aircraft rose to challenge the Americans, but AA fire shot down three Hellcats and one Avenger.

Above: Pilots receive a preflight briefing on carrier *Lexington*. On September 18 and 19, Admiral Pownall led *Lexington* and light carriers *Princeton* and *Belleau Wood* to strike Tarawa and Makin in the Gilberts, destroying 18 aircraft on Tarawa's airfield while losing four American planes to AA fire. Three picket boats and mine craft, and a transport ship were also sunk, but more important was a series of low oblique photographs taken of the lagoon side of Betio islet by *Lexington*'s planes that would prove invaluable toward the coming invasion.

Left: Commander George W. Anderson, *Yorktown*'s navigator, works out the ship's course in October 1943, the destination at that time being the former American island territory of Wake. Overrun by the Japanese on December 23, 1941, Wake was marked for special attention by the largest US Navy carrier unit to date: Task Force 14 under Rear Admiral Alfred E. Montgomery, incorporating large carriers *Essex, Yorktown*, and *Lexington*, and light carriers *Cowpens, Independence*, and *Belleau Wood*.

Right: Hellcats of VF-5 return to *Yorktown* from the first strike at Wake on October 5. When 23 of the 26 Mitsubishi A6M2 Zeros of the 252nd *Kokutai* (naval air group) came up to fight, the F6Fs shot down 15 (claiming 27), then destroyed eight more Zeros and 19 bombers on the ground. The first Zero credited to a carrier-based Hellcat fell to Ensign Robert W. Duncan of VF-5—his two victims that morning may have included Warrant Officer Toshiyuki Sueda, a nine-victory China and Pacific veteran.

Left: A Hellcat of the detachment of VF-6 assigned to light carrier *Cowpens* (CVL-25) breaks its right landing gear in a hard deck landing. Note first aid and firefighting crews standing by on catwalks and the crash barrier on right. On the afternoon of October 5, Ensign Cyrus J. Chambers and two wingmen from *Cowpens* caught a Mitsubishi G3M3 bomber of the 755th *Kokutai* over Wake and shot it down. Chambers would later add five more to that score.

Opposite: Ensign Frederick J. Joyce Jr. of *Yorktown*'s squadron VB-5 drinks some pineapple juice before taking off in his Douglas SBD-5 Dauntless to bomb Wake. After some incidents involving American airmen and gunners firing on American aircraft, the red insignia surrounds were removed due to the belief that any flash of red would be assumed Japanese. By 1944 all Allied aircraft, American or British Commonwealth, bore strictly blue-and-white national insignias.

"Jesus Christ, boys,
there's a million of 'em!
Let's get to work!"

—A Vought F4U-1A pilot of VF-17, operating
off the carrier Bunker Hill upon seeing Japanese
aircraft from Rabaul attacking Task Group 50.4,
November 11, 1943.

"Ships fightin' ships is right
and so's planes fightin'
planes, but ships fightin'
planes just ain't natural."

—An old US Navy gunner's mate during
Japanese attacks on Task Group 50.4
off Rabaul, November 11, 1943.

Opposite: The airfield and facilities on Wake burn after six strikes and 758 sorties dropped 340 tons (308.5 tonnes) of bombs on the island in two days, in addition to which the surface ships fired 520 tons (472 tonnes) of shells. Damage included a tanker sunk in the lagoon and 25 aircraft shot down, as well as numerous others destroyed on the ground, for the loss of 10 Hellcats and two Avengers. Six of the downed American fliers were rescued by the submarine *Skate*, proving the submarine's value in that role.

Opposite bottom: F6F-3s land aboard *Saratoga* after a successful air strike. When US Marines landed on Bougainville on November 1, 1943, and a Japanese naval force was repulsed in Empress Augusta Bay the following night, the Japanese assembled a larger force at Rabaul. Admiral William F. Halsey responded by dispatching *Saratoga* and light carrier *Princeton* to attack the base on November 5. No major warships were sunk, but enough suffered sufficient damage to neutralize the threat to the Bougainville beachhead.

Right: A division of four carrier pilots confer before a TBF. On November 11, *Saratoga* and *Princeton*—redesignated Task Group 50.3—were joined by Nimitz's carriers *Essex, Bunker Hill*, and *Independence* for a follow-up attack on Rabaul on November 11. The destroyer *Suzunami* was sunk and other ships damaged, but the raid's highlight was massive Japanese aerial counterattack that the carrier planes managed to fend off without a single ship being hit.

Opposite: In one of Edward Steichen's photographs aboard *Lexington*, a tractor races down the flight deck to pick up a Douglas SBD-5 Dauntless of Bombing Squadron 16 (VB-16) during Operation Galvanic (November 20–23, 1943) in the Gilbert Islands. On November 20, the 165th Regimental Combat Team (RCT) of Major General Ralph C. Smith's 27th Infantry Division landed on Makin, while the 2nd Marine Division, under Major General Julian C. Smith, moved on Tarawa Atoll's key islet of Betio.

Edward Steichen (1879–1973)

Born in Bivange, Luxembourg, in 1879, Eduard Jean Steichen was brought to the United States in 1881 and became a naturalized citizen in 1900. In 1904, he began experimenting with the new Autochrome Lumière color photographic process, and in 1911 he introduced photography into the fashion world.

In World War I, Steichen commanded the Photography Division of the American Expeditionary Force, and in World War II he became director of the Naval Aviation Photo Unit. In 1945, Steichen was made head of the Naval Photographic Institute, and his film *The Fighting Lady* won an Academy Award for Best Documentary.

Left: Lieutenant Victor Jorgensen photographed 64-year-old Lieutenant Commander Edward J. Steichen on the bridge platform of the carrier Lexington *in November 1943.*

Left: In one of Steichen's photographs, a gun director observes activities from his station in a Mark 51 director tub on *Lexington*'s "island" during operations in the Gilbert Islands in November 1943. The muzzles of a quad 40mm gun mount protrude from the AA position at right. Besides direct fire, the AA guns were sometimes used to raise water splashes in front of oncoming enemy torpedo bombers.

Left: The nine 16-inch (40.5cm) guns of the battleship *Alabama*, shown during its shakedown cruise in January 1943, made their Pacific debut bombarding Tarawa on November 20. In spite of that heavy preliminary bombardment, Rear Admiral Keiji Shibazaki's well-prepared defenses, combined with a low tide that fouled landing craft on the coral reef, resulted in the marines having to advance a quarter mile in waist-deep water under murderous gunfire.

Opposite: Marines look at a relief map of Tarawa. By the end of November 20, a relative handful of marines had reached Betio's seawall, half of the amphibious tractors that could clear the coral reef were lost, and only two of eight supporting tanks were operational, but they had advanced across half the island. On the twenty-first, the marines got a crucial double break when shelling disrupted the Japanese communication network and killed Admiral Shibazaki.

> ## "A million men cannot take Tarawa in a hundred years."
>
> —*Rear Admiral Keiji Shibazaki, garrison commander on Tarawa Atoll.*

> ## "Issue still in doubt."
>
> —*Major General Julian C. Smith to Rear Admiral Richmond Kelly Turner, commander, Fifth Amphibious Force, at the end of the first day on Tarawa, November 20, 1943.*

David M. Shoup (1906–1983)

David Monroe Shoup was born in Battle Ground, Indiana, graduated from DePauw University, and was an officer in the US Army Reserve before getting a commission in the Marine Corps in 1926, his subsequent service including Shanghai, the US Embassy in Beijing, and Iceland in 1941. Becoming the operations and training officer for the 2nd Marine Division, Shoup was an observer with the 1st Marine Division on Guadalcanal in October 1942 and was wounded while temporarily attached to the Army's 43rd Infantry Division on Rendova, New Georgia, in the summer of 1943. Given command of the 2nd Marine Regiment on November 9, 1943, Colonel Shoup led it in the assault on Tarawa, for which he was awarded the Medal of Honor. From 1960 to 1963, General Shoup served as 22nd Commandant of the Marine Corps.

"Casualties: Many. Percentage dead: Unknown. Combat efficiency: We are winning."

—*Colonel David M. Shoup, 2nd Marine Division, reporting at the end of the second day on Tarawa, November 21, 1943.*

Left: A navy corpsman administers blood plasma to a wounded marine on the pier at Betio on November 22. That afternoon 1st Battalion, 6th Marines advanced across the southern part of the islet to the east side of the airfield. Japanese counterattacks that night climaxed with a last desperate banzai charge that ended with about 325 Japanese dead. The last resistance was overcome the following day.

Below: SBD-5s and a Grumman J2F amphibian occupy Betio's airstrip, behind the graves of two marines who died to take it. After three days of taking the three-mile-long (5km) islet, strongpoint by strongpoint, the final cost of securing Betio on November 23 totaled 990 marine and 687 navy personnel killed, along with 4,713 defenders. Only 17 Japanese and 129 Korean laborers survived as prisoners.

Above: A tractor re-spots an F6F-3 of fighter squadron VF-30 on the deck of light carrier *Monterey* (CVL-26) in November 1943. The "F" designator issued to early Hellcats was later removed, leaving only the two-digit number. In theory, each numbered plane was assigned to a specific pilot. In practice, carrier pilots flew whatever plane was available for the mission— seldom, if ever, flying the same one twice.

Below left: F6F-3 Hellcats and TBF-1 Avengers of Air Group 30 line up for takeoff from *Monterey*'s flight deck. Originally laid down as the light cruiser Dayton (CL-78) but completed as a light carrier (CVL-26), *Monterey*'s planes supported the landings on Makin and Majuro, as well as air strikes on Nauru and Kavieng in December. Among its crewmen during those operations in the Gilbert and Solomon Islands was future president, Ensign Gerald R. Ford.

Below right: Army troops man a .50-caliber antiaircraft machine gun emplacement on Makin beach shortly after securing the island on November 24. The 165th Regimental Combat Team encountered much less intense resistance from Makin's 800 defenders, killing 396 Japanese and taking three prisoners, along with 101 Korean laborers, for the loss of only 66 dead and 185 wounded or injured. The US Navy supporting them from offshore fared much worse.

Opposite: Lieutenant Junior Grade Eugene R. Hanks poses in his F6F-3 for Edward Steichen's camera aboard *Lexington*. On November 23, Zeros of the 252nd *Kokutai* tried to bomb and strafe the Americans on Makin, only to be intercepted by VF-16 Hellcats. The Japanese claimed five victories and five probables for the loss of nine planes, while VF-16 claimed 17 Zeros without loss—five of them credited to "Five-Shot Hanks."

Left: Landing Signal Officer (LSO), Lieutenant John W. Clark, stands by to guide a plane in during the Gilberts campaign. On Tarawa, the navy learned that "softening up" operations were not enough in themselves. While the army's 27th Infantry Division suffered relatively low casualties "takin' Makin," the navy's 697 dead included 43 in a turret fire aboard battleship *Mississippi* on November 20, and 644 more men lost when escort carrier *Liscombe Bay* was torpedoed and sunk by Japanese submarine *I-175* on the twenty-fourth.

Below: The forward superstructure, fire control, and antiaircraft guns of battleship *Alabama*, which were brought into play fighting off nocturnal torpedo attacks by G4M2 Bettys on November 26. Also up that night was Lieutenant Commander Edward "Butch" O'Hare, now commanding VF-2 on *Enterprise*, as part of a team of two Hellcats and one radar-equipped Avenger trying to intercept the raiders. O'Hare was hit by a Betty gunner, however, and killed in action.

Right: A disabled Zero sits on Kwajalein's airstrip in the wake of the American carrier strikes. During the December attacks, Kwajalein's depleted 252nd *Kokutai* was reinforced by elements of carrier *Zuikaku*'s air group, which had previously operated over Rabaul. One of its veterans, Warrant Officer Saburo Saito, was credited with four American fighters during the raids, one of his victims possibly being "Wendy" Wendorf of VF-16. Saito survived the war with 18 victories.

Left: A plane director brings a landed Hellcat down *Lexington*'s flight deck. After the Gilberts operation, *Lexington* raided Kwajalein in the Marshalls on December 4, sinking cargo ship *Kembu Maru* and damaging two cruisers, while its pilots claimed 30 victories. Two Zeros and a quarter claim on a Betty went to Ensign Edward G. Wendorf of VF-16 before he was wounded. After crash-landing aboard *Lexington*, Wendorf's shot-up F6F was displayed at the Grumman plant to show what punishment it could take.

Arthur W. Radford (1896–1973)

Born in Chicago and graduating from the US Naval Academy in 1916, Arthur William Radford served in World War I and qualified as a pilot in 1921. In 1941 he was Director of Aviation Training and also assigned Commander Edward Steichen's unit to operate under his Training Literature Division. In July 1943, Radford entered the war as commander of Carrier Division 11, supporting the invasions of Baker Island, Tarawa, and Makin, during which he also helped develop the navy's night fighter tactics. He subsequently commanded Task Groups 58.4 and 38.4. He commanded the Pacific Fleet during the Korean War, and as chairman of the Joint Chiefs of Staff in 1955–57, Radford promoted the Polaris missile submarine program.

Left: Steichen photographed aviation mechanics working on an F6F-3's Pratt & Whitney R-2800 engine between strikes on Mili and Kwajalein. In spite of the Marshalls raids' general success, G4M2 Bettys harassed the Fifth Fleet throughout the night of December 4, one scoring a torpedo hit on *Lexington* that jammed its steering gear and killed nine men. After repairs in Bremerton, Washington, *Lexington* rejoined Task Force 58 as Vice Admiral Marc Mitscher's flagship on March 8, 1944.

Above: A view from *Monterey*'s bridge shows the crane and Hellcats on the forward flight deck. On December 25, carriers *Monterey* and *Bunker Hill,* making up Task Group 50.2 under Rear Admiral Frederick C. Sherman, ventured into the Solomons to give the Japanese base at Kavieng a Christmas surprise, sinking the transport *Tenryu Maru*, setting transport *Kiyosumi Maru* on fire, and damaging two minesweepers. The task group fended off Japanese air attacks throughout the night.

Right: Marines, with inflatable life vests near at hand, pass the time playing gin rummy aboard a transport bound for Kwajalein Atoll. The Japanese defense in the Marshalls relied heavily on six widely scattered island airfields, but a series of air strikes by Admiral Raymond A. Spruance's Fifth Fleet and the Seventh Air Force swiftly eliminated them. Kwajalein was then subjected to a devastating "Spruance Haircut" and "Mitscher Shampoo" before the marines landed on January 31, 1944.

Below: Wrecked Japanese landing craft and other small vessels litter the beachhead area on Kawajalein. Deciding to neutralize and then simply bypass other Marshall Island bases, Operation Flintlock involved Major General Harry Schmidt's 4th Marine Division landing on Roi and Namur islets in Kwajalein Atoll on January 31, and Army Major General Charles H. Corlett's 7th Infantry Division landing on Kwajalein Island on February 1. Additionally, Majuro, 220 miles (354km) to the southeast, was seized and turned into a key air base.

Left: Japanese dead await burial after the battle for Kwajalein. Most of Rear Admiral Monzo Akiyama's 6th Base Force was stationed on other islands, such as Jaluit, Mille, Maloelap, and Wotje, which the Americans did not invade, and less than half of his personnel were combat trained. Fighting primarily at the beachhead cost the Japanese 7,870 dead and 105 captured in the course of unsuccessfully defending Kwajalein, Roi, and Namur, compared to 372 Americans killed and 1,592 wounded.

Below: Grumman TBF-1 Avengers of VT-10 are brought topside for launching from *Enterprise*'s deck. On February 17 and 18, *Enterprise* joined its more modern *Essex*- and *Independence*-class cousins in an attack on Truk in the Caroline Islands, a superb natural anchorage the Japanese had taken from the Germans in World War I and developed into their largest staging base in the Central Pacific.

January 1944 Allied forces assault Monte Cassino on January 16, only to be stalemated until May 18. On January 22, the Allies move 55 miles (88km) up the Italian coast, to land at Anzio and Nettuno, but are again stalemated until May.

January 27, 1944 Soviet forces decisively break the Siege of Leningrad, ending 872 days of German blockade in which more than a million Russian soldiers and civilians were killed or missing, the latter mostly dying of starvation and disease.

"Those Grummans are beautiful planes. If they could cook, I'd marry one."

—Grumman F6F-3 Hellcat pilot Lieutenant Junior Grade Eugene Valencia of VF-9, carrier Essex, after engaging six Zeros and shooting down three of them over Truk on February 17, 1944.

Right: Ship's mascot Scrappy poses with Aviation Machinist's Mate Third Class Robert L. Brown in the flag-bedecked cockpit of a VF-5 F6F-3 aboard *Yorktown* after the Truk strike. Truk had enjoyed a fearsome reputation, primarily because of the secrecy surrounding it. That mystique was shattered on February 17, 1944, in an air battle that virtually annihilated the Japanese and made aces of numerous Hellcat pilots, including VF-5's Bob Duncan, who claimed four Zeros that day.

February 20–25, 1944 *"Big Week," an Allied bombing effort aimed at inflicting attrition on the Luftwaffe, costs the RAF 131 bombers, and the USAAF 261 bombers and 33 fighters, but the Germans lose 355 fighters and about 100 pilots.*

March 6, 1944 *After two aborts, the Eighth Air Force makes its first massed daylight raid on Berlin, provoking another confrontation with the Luftwaffe that costs the Americans 69 bombers and 11 fighters, and the Germans 160 aircraft.*

Right: F6F-3s of VF-10 prepare to catapult from *Enterprise*. In the course of four missions on February 17, VF-10's pilots were credited with 23 Zeros, three Nakajima A6M2-N floatplane fighters, and an Aichi D3A2 dive bomber for the loss of three Hellcats, two of whose pilots were rescued. The one fatality, Ensign Linton Cox, was downed by an A6M2-N of the 902nd *Kokutai*, which lost the last of its eight floatplanes on the eighteenth.

Below: *New Jersey*, Admiral Spruance's Fifth Fleet flagship. Off Truk, *New Jersey* and sister battleship *Iowa* pursued the fleeing light training cruiser *Katori* and destroyers *Maikaze* and *Nowake*. Heavy cruisers sank *Katori*, while *Maikaze* narrowly missed the battlewagons with a torpedo before being sunk by their 5-inch (12.5cm) secondary batteries. *Nowake* escaped, but two light cruisers, four destroyers, and 40 other ships were sunk at Truk, along with 270 aircraft destroyed, for the American loss of 25 planes and torpedo damage to carrier *Intrepid*.

Below: Crewmen clean a 20mm antiaircraft gun emplaced at Eniwetok Atoll naval anchorage. Engebi fell in six hours on February 18, but it took the Army's 106th Infantry Regiment from the eighteenth to the nineteenth to secure Eniwetok Island. Parry Island took 900 tons (816.5 tonnes) of battleship shelling before the 22nd Marines landed there on the twenty-second. The entire atoll was secured on the twenty-third, having cost 262 American dead and 77 missing, compared to 2,677 Japanese killed.

Right: A B-25 of the Seventh Air Force prepares for a sortie in the Marshalls. Once Kwajalein and Eniwetok were secured, bombers of the "Pineapple Air Force," as tho Seventh was also called, flew harassing raids against the bypassed islands still in Japanese hands, such as Maloelap, Jaluit, and Wotje. Aside from a diminishing number of operational fighters, floatplanes, and flying boats, the most consistent danger came from antiaircraft guns.

Opposite: A mechanic works on a Vought F4U-1A Corsair of VMF-223 on Green Island. On February 15, Battalions 30, 35, and 37 of the 4th New Zealand Brigade, closely accompanied by combat engineers of the 93rd Naval Construction Battalion, landed on Green Island. Once secured, the island group acquired a PT boat base and airfields that served as both transit points and bases from which to raid Rabaul and other Japanese holdouts in the Bismarck Archipelago.

Below: Armorers install .50-caliber machine guns in a Vought F4U-1A Corsair of VMF-223 on Green Island in May 1944. Between May 22 and June 10, 1944, Charles A. Lindbergh visited Green Island as part of his program to extend fighters' operational ranges, which he had previously applied to the Lockheed P-38 and also wished to do with the Corsair. Lindbergh also flew 13 combat missions with VMF-223, before alarmed authorities ordered the belligerent civilian stateside.

Battle for Bypassed Bougainville

When marines stormed ashore in Empress Augusta Bay on November 1, 1943, Bougainville Island was a key toward controlling the Bismarck Archipelago in the upper Solomon Islands. By early 1944, however, with the once-powerful Japanese air and naval base at Rabaul hammered into near irrelevance, Bougainville became a bypassed sideshow as US Army troops took over from the marines to complete the job of safeguarding the airfield established at Torokina and finishing off the island's remaining defenders.

As things turned out, what remained was most of Bougainville's garrison, and on March 10 it made its first serious attempt to drive the Americans out, as 1,300 Japanese assaulted and seized Hill 260 from the 148th Regiment of the 23rd "Americal" Division. The 148th counterattacked, and by March 28 it had retaken the hill, killing 580 Japanese in the process. From then on, the Allies made a series of offensives to wrest further ground from the enemy. One such advance, by the 25th Infantry Regiment along the Numa Numa Trail to the mouth of the Mavavia River in April, marked the first offensive use of black American soldiers during World War II. Although eliminated as a threat to Torokina Airfield, from which the Allies continued to raid Rabaul, the surviving Japanese holed up in the jungle hills of Bougainville for the rest of the war.

Above: Defensive positions of the recently arrived black 25th Regiment, 93rd Infantry Division line Hill 260 in April 1944. After gaining experience by training and working alongside the Americal Division's 148th Infantry, the 25th advanced along the Numa Numa Trail on April 2, and on April 24 its troops cleared 1,000 yards (914.5m) of beachfront along the mouth of the Mavavia River, killing 47 Japanese and taking one prisoner, for the loss of 13 men killed and 13 wounded.

Left: A US Navy construction battalion lays steel Marsden matting for a new bomber airfield on Bougainville between December 15 and 19, 1943.

Right: A Curtiss P-40N Kittyhawk of the Royal New Zealand Air Force is photographed from Garnett Tower as it takes off from Fighter Strip No.1 of Torokina Airfield.

Below: A 4.2-inch mortar crew of the 82nd Chemical Battalion pounds a Japanese position on Bougainville in April 1944. Designed to fire chemical agents but used only to fire high explosive rounds during the war, the 4.2-inch (10.5cm) mortar was an invaluable infantry support weapon.

"The headlong flight of the enemy at the appearance of the Aitape and Hollandia Task Forces was an event unparalleled in the history of our campaign against the Japanese."

—Lieutenant General Walter Krueger, commander, US Sixth Army.

Left: Crewmen muster in formation on *Lexington*'s flight deck before manning their stations for the Hollandia operation. The struggle for New Guinea had cost 16,850 American and 17,000 Australian casualties, but 123,000 of the 180,000 men the Japanese committed to the campaign died there—a great many of them of disease, malnutrition, or other causes after retreating into the jungle and being bypassed by the advancing Allies.

Marc A. Mitscher (1887–1947)

Vice Admiral Marc Andrew Mitscher, here awarding a medal to a *Lexington*'s crewman for his contribution to the 1944 Hollandia operation, was born in Hillsboro, Wisconsin, raised in Oklahoma City, and graduated from the US Naval Academy in 1910. On June 2, 1916, he became naval aviator No. 33. He commanded the carrier *Hornet* during the Tokyo raid and the Battle of Midway until relieved on June 30, 1942. On March 21, 1944, he took command of Task Force 58, the fast carrier element of the Fifth Fleet. After Hollandia, Task Force 58 completed the neutralization of Truk as a base between April 29 and 30.

Right: Photographed at Nadzab, Lockheed P-38J-15 *Marge* of the 9th Squadron, 49th Fighter Group was named after Marjorie Vattendahl, fiancée of Captain Richard Ira Bong, who had shot down three Japanese aircraft on April 12, 1944, raising his score to 27 to exceed that of World War I American ace of aces Edward Rickenbacker. Promoted to major, Bong was sent home to participate in a war bond drive, but returned to action later in the year.

Below: Carrier *Yorktown* and another warship of Rear Admiral Joseph J. "Jocko" Clark's Task Group 58.1 heads for Hollandia in early April 1944. The US Sixth Army, supported by Navy Task Force 58, landed at Hollandia on April 22 and secured the base for Allied use four days later. At neighboring Aitape, the 163rd Regimental Combat Team landed on April 22, and secured Tadji Airfield the next day.

Left: When photographed on Hollandia with his new P-38J-15 Lightning, Major Thomas B. McGuire, commander of the 431st Squadron, 475th Fighter Group, had scored his eighteenth victory on May 18, 1944. McGuire would down three more opponents in *Pudgy III*. His total was 38, just two behind Dick Bong, when his plane stalled and fell into a fatal spin during a dogfight on January 7, 1945. McGuire was posthumously awarded the Medal of Honor.

Chapter 4

Hell is Upon Us

The Allied offensive gathers momentum

Opposite: A photograph by Edward Steichen shows an American battleship unleashing a salvo at sea. Both sides committed their most modern battleships to the Battle of Leyte Gulf, but the only time the "heavy hitters" met was at Surigao Strait on the night of October 24, when the ungainly old Japanese *Yamashiro* and *Fuso* rushed to their doom against a waiting line that included the equally elderly American battlewagons *West Virginia, Tennessee, California, Mississippi, Maryland,* and *Pennsylvania.*

While the Americans were on the march in the Pacific, the Japanese tried to maintain their momentum in Asia. On March 8 the Japanese army assaulted the Bengali town of Imphal, only to be defeated by its British and Indian defenders. A similar battle at Kohima, fought from April 4 to June 22, also ended in costly defeat. On June 6 the British 77th Chindit Brigade assaulted Mogaung, Burma, securing it on the twenty-seventh. By July 3, the British Fourteenth Army, under Lieutenant General William Slim, was ready to carry the fight into Burma.

On June 15, US Marines landed on Saipan, and in history's greatest carrier duel, the Battle of the Philippine Sea on June 19–20, the US Navy tore the heart out of Japan's carrier air arm. On the island, however, the Japanese put up a desperate defense that climaxed with a massive suicidal banzai charge and the suicides en masse of soldiers and civilians alike off the cliffs of Marpi Point. With Saipan, Guam, and Tinian secured, the Americans established air bases from which new Boeing B-29s could bomb targets on the Japanese home islands. These developments, in the wake of the fall of the Marianas, led a Japanese cabinet minister to remark, "Hell is upon us." On November 24, the Marianas-based B-29s made their first strike on Tokyo.

American landings in the Philippines, on October 20, precipitated history's largest sea engagement, the Battle of Leyte Gulf, which left Japan's once-mighty

Right: A Vought F4U-1A that was badly damaged by antiaircraft fire during a raid on one of the Japanese bases bypassed in Admiral Chester Nimitz's and General Douglas MacArthur's island-hopping campaigns. It awaits either repair or cannibalization for usable spare parts on Green Island in May 1944. By that time, the Solomons and eastern New Guinea had been reduced to backwaters as the Allied offensives forged west toward the Marianas and the Philippines.

Opposite: Guided by his colleagues, the driver of a Jeep very carefully tows a 37mm antitank gun ashore from a Higgins-built LVT(I) (landing craft vehicle, infantry) during a US Army training exercise in Australia. The exercise was organized by General Douglas MacArthur to prepare the troops for his planned campaign to seize a series of bases along the northern New Guinea coast before going on to capture a string of strategically important islands across the Southwest Pacific leading to the Philippines.

Above: Soldiers of the 32nd Infantry Division's 126th Regimental Combat Team prepare to board ship for Saidor, New Guinea. After Fifth Air Force strikes neutralized the airfield, the 13,000 Americans, commanded by Brigadier General Clarence A. Martin, landed on January 2, 1944, and soon secured Saidor, killing 119 Japanese and taking 13 prisoners while losing 40 men dead, 11 wounded, and 16 missing.

William Slim (1891–1970)

Born in Bishopston, near Bristol, William Slim was wounded twice during World War I and a third time in Ethiopia in 1941, later serving in North Africa before arriving in India amid Britain's Burmese debacle in March 1942. He rose to command the Fourteenth Army and under his leadership, as well as the training of Major General Orde Wingate, British Commonwealth troops learned to beat the Japanese soldier at his own game. After foiling Japanese attempts to invade India in the Battles of the Admin Box (February 4–23, 1944), Imphal (March 8–July 3), and Kohima (April 4–June 22), Slim's troops prepared to go over to the offensive and retake Burma.

War under the Waves

The US Pacific Fleet had 21 submarines when the Japanese attacked Pearl Harbor, but in the wake of that disaster it wasted little time in deploying them with orders to carry out unrestricted submarine warfare on the enemy. Their torpedoes were initially handicapped by faulty firing pins, but once that flaw was determined and remedied in late 1943, the submarines' successes became disproportionate to their numbers.

In August 1942 the first radar was installed in an American submarine, and early in 1943 they adopted a variation on German wolf pack tactics, although the smaller Japanese convoys required fewer submarines and their captains were given more flexibility than their German counterparts. In 1944, oilers received high priority, and on April 13 Rear Admiral Charles A. Lockwood ordered his sub skippers to eliminate their traditional nemeses, destroyers, 39 of which they sank by the end of the war.

Although submariners only constituted 1.6 percent of US Navy personnel, they accounted for 54 percent of the 10 million tons (9 million tonnes) of Japanese military and merchant shipping sunk during the war. The price they paid was high: 52 submarines and 3,505 crewmen—one in five submariners—did not return from Pacific patrols.

Edward Steichen photographed aspects of life aboard the *Gato*-class boat *Cero*. As flagship to Captain Charles B. "Swede" Momsen, *Cero* led the navy's first wolf pack along with *Shad* and *Grayback*, whose standard tactic was to attack Japanese convoys from aft and both flanks. Besides sinking 18,159 tons (16,473.5 tonnes) of enemy shipping, *Cero* supplied guerrillas in the Philippines, rescued downed airmen, and earned seven battle stars in the course of eight wartime patrols.

Above: A crewman emerges to take up station on *Cero*'s conning tower while the surfaced submarine takes in oxygen, runs on its diesel engine, and recharges its batteries.

Above: A lookout scans the sky for enemy planes, as well as the horizon for enemy ships, from his platform on *Cero*'s periscope sheers.

Left: A chief petty officer standing beside the access ladder, with diving controls at left, mans the submarine control station.

Below: Charles Fenno Jacobs photographed officers in *Cero*'s wardroom; (from left) Commander David C. White, Lieutenant Commander David H. McClintock, and Lieutenant Charles D. Nace being served by the submarine's black steward's mate.

Charles Fenno Jacobs (1905–1973)

Born in Waltham, Massachusetts, Charles Fenno Jacobs was described by his sister Frances as a redheaded scourge who dropped out of eighth grade and joined the merchant marine. After marrying the first of three wives, Jacobs took up photography for real estate salesmen and went on to be the photographer for *Life, National Geographic, US Camera,* and *Fortune* magazines, as well as for the Farm Security Administration. In World War II, Edward Steichen invited him to join his Naval Aviation Photo Unit, and Jacobs became adept at capturing the human interest in factories and aboard ships. After the war he became the European photographer for *Fortune* magazine and was also a noted wine connoisseur, gastronome, and cook before his death from heart disease in Englewood, New Jersey, in 1973.

Left: Members of the Women's Auxiliary Corps, the Indian equivalent of Britain's Auxiliary Territorial Service, parade in uniforms dictated on tradition and conviction—most in full British-style uniform and a few eschewing hats and wearing their tunics over a camouflage version of the traditional sari. Performing the same duties as all women in the Allied armies, Indian women freed up thousands of men to defend their country against the looming threat of Japanese invasion in 1944.

> ## "When you first met him, you thought he was a maniac; after a week you would have died for him."
>
> *—A Chindit, on Major General Orde Wingate.*

Opposite: Lieutenant Colonel Robert T. Smith and Colonel Philip Cochran of the 1st Air Commando Group confer with Major General Orde Charles Wingate, the legendary unconventional warfare specialist who trained special long-range jungle penetration brigades called the Chindits to prove that the British could acclimate themselves to jungle fighting, and sent them to raid the Japanese in Burma throughout 1943. Wingate coordinated his Chindit operations with the 1st Air Commando in early 1944.

Above: An Indian crew mans antiaircraft guns around the air base of the 12th Bombardment Group (Medium) at Fenny. Transferred to the Tenth Air Force from the Twelfth in Italy in February 1944, the 12th Group flew B-25s to strike at Japanese installations and disrupt transport and communication routes. Its planes also air-dropped supplies to the British defending Imphal and Kohima in April 1944.

> ## "This ain't fighting bloody Japs; it's fighting bloody nature."
>
> *—A British soldier on the war in Burma.*

May–June 1944 Allies break out of the Anzio beachhead on May 25 and take Rome on June 5. On June 6, British, American, and Canadian forces land in Normandy and establish five beachheads in France.

June 22, 1944 The Red Army launches Operation Bagration, which by July 4 retakes Minsk and inflicts 300,000 casualties on German Army Group Center.

June 25–July 9, 1944 *The Battle of Tali-Ihantala, in which, at terrible cost, the Finnish army stops a Soviet offensive and convinces Josef Stalin to seek separate peace terms from Helsinki, which capitulates conditionally on September 5.*

July–August 1944 *Americans at St. Lô and British at Caen achieve breakouts in Normandy. After a failed German counteroffensive at Mortain and the destruction of much of the German army in France at Falaise, Paris is liberated on August 25.*

Left: (from left) Lieutenant Colonel Robert T. Smith, leader of the 1st Air Commando's bomber squadron, poses before his B-25H *Barbie III* with the group's cocommanders, Colonels John Alison and Phil Cochran, at Hailkandi, India. A former American Volunteer Group ace, Smith was awarded the Silver Star, Distinguished Flying Cross, and Air Medal for his work with the 1st Air Commando. Cartoonist Milton Caniff modeled his comic-strip hero, Flip Corkin, from *Terry and the Pirates*, on Cochran.

Below: Lieutenant Ralph Lanning's B-25H-1 *Erotic Edna* of the 1st Air Commando Group, armed with a 75mm cannon for attacking ground targets, accompanies R. T. Smith on a support mission in Burma. Lanning and his plane were also used as a transport by General Wingate, who was tragically killed in another B-25, along with nine Americans, in a crash in northern India on March 24, 1944.

"Please be assured that we will go with you boys,
any place, any time, any where."

—*Major General Orde Wingate to the 1st Air Commando Group,
which adopted the last six words as its unit motto.*

Satoshi Anabuki (1921–2005)

The Japanese army's leading ace, Satoshi Anabuki came from a farming family, but at an early age entered the Army Youth Preparatory Flight Program and graduated from the Tokyo Army Aviation School in 1938. Flying Nakajima Ki.27s (Allied codename "Nate") and Ki.43s ("Oscar") with the 3rd *Chutai* (squadron), 50th *Koku Sentai* (air regiment), he distinguished himself over Burma until he was injured colliding with a Consolidated B-24 on October 8, 1943. Sent home, he nevertheless claimed four F6F Hellcats in the course of ferry flights to the Philippines, and a Boeing B-29 for his fifty-first victory, although 30 Allied planes destroyed or damaged is a more likely total.

Tracks of the Cat

The Consolidated PBY-1 Catalina flying boat was an advanced design when it joined the US Navy as a patrol bomber in 1937. It was slow and ungainly when World War II broke out, but remained reliable, easy to fly, long-ranging, and remarkably versatile. In consequence, at least 4,051 were built in the United States, Canada, and even the Soviet Union, making it the most-produced flying boat in history. An amphibious version, the PBY-5A, featured retractable wheeled landing gear.

PBYs served throughout the war in antisubmarine and maritime patrolling, search and rescue, and transport duties, but on many occasions the "Cat" proved to have claws, as first demonstrated on October 15, 1942, when

Major Jack R. Cram, pilot of Major General Roy S. Geiger's transport PBY-5A *Blue Goose*, improvised an underwing rig to carry two 2,000-pound (907kg) torpedoes, departed Guadalcanal's Henderson Field to attack a Japanese troop convoy, and scored two hits that sank the transport *Sasago Maru*, for which he was awarded the Navy Cross. Over the next three years specialized "Black Cats," equipped with magnetic anomaly detection gear, bombs, and torpedoes, carried out nocturnal attacks on whatever enemy craft they encountered. By the end of the war, these aggressively flown PBYs were credited with sinking 112,700 tons (102,239.5 tonnes) of Japanese merchant shipping.

Left: An amphibious PBY-5A of Patrol Squadron VP-3 shows the retractable nosewheel that distinguished it from the PBY-5 and earlier flying boat variants.

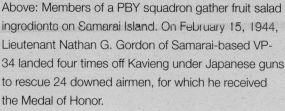

Above: Members of a PBY squadron gather fruit salad ingredients on Samarai Island. On February 15, 1944, Lieutenant Nathan G. Gordon of Samarai-based VP-34 landed four times off Kavieng under Japanese guns to rescue 24 downed airmen, for which he received the Medal of Honor.

Above: Ground crewmen work on a Black Cat's gun observation blister at a Pacific island naval repair base in April 1945. The blister's glazing could be retracted to fire a .30-caliber machine gun if the PBY came under air attack.

Right: A crew member mans the radio compartment in a "Black Cat" PBY during a nocturnal prowl from Samarai Island in Milne Bay, New Guinea, in 1944.

"The squadron takes pardonable pride in the fact that virtually every major contact with Jap surface forces was first developed by search airplanes from VP-54."

—*Excerpt from the war diary of VP-54.*

Above: A Tenth Air Force bomber pounds Japanese positions beside the Irrawaddy River near Myitkyina. On May 17, 1944, a mixed Sino-American force, centered on Brigadier General Frank D. Merrill's jungle-trained 5307th Composite Unit (Provisional), better known as Force Galahad or Merrill's Marauders, attacked Myitkyina. Fighting dragged on until August 10, when the last 600 survivors of the 4,600 Japanese defenders slipped away, leaving the exhausted Allies with an important airfield for their next advance in Burma.

Right: Staff Sergeant Joseph Heilberger checks his camera on Guadalcanal on March 13, 1944, prior to shipping out on a frontline assignment. Besides the photojournalists and Edward Steichen's picked team, many army, navy, and marine units had their own photographic sections, recording their activities as well as providing pictures that could provide useful intelligence. Their often hazardous sorties into harm's way added to the pictorial record after the war.

Right: Pilots of the Chinese American Composite Wing discuss the next day's coming operation. After training in India, the 3rd and 5th Fighter Groups of the CACW were ready to join the Fourteenth Air Force's fight against *Ichi-Go* in early 1944. Among its many successful pilots was China's World War II ace of aces, First Lieutenant Wang Kwang-fu of the 7th Squadron, 3rd Fighter Group, credited with six and a half Japanese planes.

Below: Sergeant Elmer J. Pence adds a new Japanese flag indicating an aerial victory to a Curtiss P-40K, No. 255 of the 26th Squadron, 51st Fighter Group. Transferred from the Tenth to the Fourteenth Air Force in September 1943 to guard the "Hump" air bases flying transports over the Himalayas, the group claimed 34 victories in December. In April it joined the 23rd Fighter Group in Chennault's effort to stem the Japanese advance.

Below: Troops attend religious services before a makeshift altar on Bougainville. Trained to conduct often improvised rites along with whatever specialties their branch of service required—including parachuting—military chaplains dealt with servicemen's personal problems, assisted in caring for the wounded, administered last rites, and wrote to the families of the deceased. Of 8,896 American chaplains—including 5,620 Protestant, 2,278 Catholic, and 243 Jewish—77 died in the line of duty during World War II.

Left: Pilots of Navy Scouting Squadron VS-51, based on the island of Samoa, discuss plans for a patrol over South Pacific waters. Equipped with SBD-5 Dauntless dive bombers, VS-51 was engaged primarily in antisubmarine activities around Samoa from mid-1944 onward, securing vital American shipping lanes for the offensive operations to come. Japanese aircraft were equally, but less effectively, active against American submarines behind their lines.

Right: F4U-1A Corsairs of VMF-111 undergo maintenance on a base in the Gilbert Islands. While the main Allied effort closed inexorably on Japan, units such as VMF-111 kept the bypassed Japanese bases from reviving their strength with constant attacks, using bombs as heavy as 1,000 pounds (453.5kg). One of VMF-111's Corsairs, "Ole 122," made 178 flights, including 100 combat missions in the Marshalls, logging 80,000 air miles (128,747km) without a major overhaul.

Far left: The adage that "sex sells" was applied toward grabbing and holding a reader's attention in instruction manuals and posted bulletins throughout the US armed services, and seemed to strike a particularly resonant chord in remote Pacific bases. The lightly libidinous humor in this typical double entendre serves a serious purpose on an island teeming with biting and stinging insects, including malaria-spreading mosquitoes capable of putting a serviceman out of service.

Left: Another variation of "sex sells" is seen in the "light" reading matter that a member of the new battleship *Missouri*'s crew peruses during an off hour in August 1944. The booklet *What About Girls?* was published by the Public Affairs Committee and is meant to be earnestly educational, but the more important thing to a bored, off-duty sailor is that it is reading matter at all.

Left: Off-shift crewmen have a poker game in their quarters aboard the battleship *New Mexico* during a lull in operations in mid-1944. Whether or not it was approved of, whether or not the men admitted there were serious stakes involved, whether or not one survived to spend his winnings, gambling has been a part of the fighting man's arsenal against boredom since time immemorial.

Right: Crewmen aboard an LCI (landing craft, infantry) indulge in some deep-sea fishing during a break in their training exercises while their cook, holding the craft's canine mascot, Trixie, observes their progress with hopeful expectations. Whether successful or not, such activities relieved the long periods of boredom aboard ship between the moments of terror that attended their commitment to an island landing.

Below: Soldiers train in Australia for further US Army landings off western New Guinea. They landed at Aitape on May 15, 1944, and on Wakde Island on the eighteenth. On May 27 the troops landed on Biak, to find the toughest fighting further inland, in a model for many future Japanese island defenses. Nevertheless, by June 22, American aircraft were operating from both Owi and Mokmer airfields on Biak.

Below: A sailor operates a transmitter/receiver during a landing exercise to perfect amphibious warfare communications for the coming Marianas campaign. From Tarawa onward, the navy and marines honed their skills in coordinating the efforts of naval, air, artillery, and armored assets to assist the riflemen who had to make the deadly first steps from the troopships to the landing craft conveying them to hostile shores.

Below: Staff Sergeant Robert S. Smith, a veteran of bombing missions in B-17s and B-24s, demonstrates gunnery in a practice turret at a base on New Guinea. With Wakde Island secured, on May 27, 1944, the first B-24s departed its improved airfield to attack Mindanao in the Philippines. The subsequent taking of air bases on the islands of Noemfoor and Morotai brought the Japanese oil refineries at Balikpapan, Borneo, within range of the Liberators.

Left: A "Jive" band assembled from musically talented crewmen entertains sunbathing sailors aboard battleship *New Mexico* as the US Fifth Fleet approaches the Marianas. Engaged in Atlantic neutrality patrols when the Japanese attacked Pearl Harbor, it supported numerous Pacific invasions, including Kiska on July 21, 1943. *New Mexico* commenced operations in the Marianas by bombarding Tinian on June 14, 1944, Saipan on the fifteenth, and Guam on the sixteenth.

Right: An LVT-4 (landing vehicle, tracked) enters the water in an exercise preceding its combat debut, the invasion of Saipan. Developed from a civilian swamp vehicle invented by Donald Roebling in 1935, the amphibious LVTs provided the marines with an extraordinary degree of mobility, and 18,621 were built in total. The LVT-4 Water Buffalo, featuring a stern ramp, was the most-produced model, 8,351 being used by US and British forces.

"Oh, that! What'd they give me a medal for that for? Everybody was doing that! You see a couple of your guys cut down . . . what else do you do?"

—Photographer's Mate Second Class Paul D. Guttman, on learning that he had been awarded the Silver Star—55 years later— for rescuing two wounded marines under fire on Saipan on June 16, 1944.

Above: Marines warily look toward the front line during fighting on Saipan. On June 15, 1944, the 2nd and 4th Marine Divisions of the 5th Amphibious Corps landed and threw back a Japanese counterattack, and the following day the 27th Infantry Division landed and seized Aslito Airfield, also repulsing a counterattack. Afterward, Lieutenant General Yoshitsugu Saito conducted a stubborn fighting retreat into the interior of Saipan, contesting every American gain as long as possible, until his 43rd Division ran out of territory to defend.

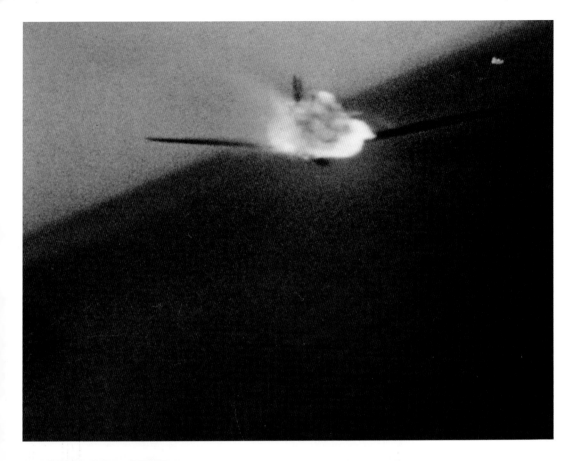

"Hell, this is like an old-time turkey shoot!"

—A fighter pilot aboard carrier Lexington after the first day of the Battle of the Philippine Sea, also known thereafter as the Great Marianas Turkey Shoot.

Left: A Japanese plane set ablaze by an F6F-3 typifies the fate of 326—for the loss of only 23 Americans—during the Battle of the Philippine Sea on June 19, 1944. Vice Admiral Jisaburo Ozawa's plan to catch the Fifth Fleet between his nine aircraft carriers and ground-based planes in the Marianas was brilliant in concept, but in practice Marc Mitscher's 15 carriers had neutralized the island air bases before the carrier planes arrived.

Above: Sailors aboard the destroyer *Halford* man their 20mm and 40mm guns as Japanese aircraft slip through the cordon of Hellcats, only to encounter a wall of antiaircraft fire. Of the four waves of Japanese carrier planes, the survivors of the last three got close enough to attack carriers *Enterprise, Princeton, Bunker Hill,* and *Wasp,* but none scored a hit.

Above: Battleship *New Mexico*'s crew fire one of its five-inch (12.5cm) guns during the Marianas campaign. After bombarding Saipan before and during the landings, *New Mexico* escorted the troopships throughout the operation, providing protection against land or carrier-launched air raids during the Battle of the Philippine Sea.

"I pulled out, easing down at about 300 feet [91m] and was immediately taken under fire by all sorts of ships— battleships, cruisers, and destroyers."

—*Lieutenant Commander James D. Ramage, leader of SBD-5-equipped VB-10 off carrier* Enterprise, *recounting the attack on the Japanese fleet on June 20, 1944, in which his bomb fell just aft of carrier* Ryuho, *causing minor damage. He landed on carrier* Yorktown *that night.*

Right: Lieutenant Junior Grade George T. Glacken and his gunner, Leo Boulanger, take part in the April 1944 Hollandia operation in their SBD-5 of *Lexington*'s Bomber Squadron VB-16. During the strike on the retiring Japanese fleet on June 20, Glacken was credited with two enemy planes, bombing an aircraft carrier, and making a successful night landing aboard *Lexington*, subsequently receiving the Navy Cross for his "brilliant airmanship, aggressive fighting spirit, and unwavering devotion to duty."

Above: A US Navy ship performs a burial at sea off Saipan following the Battle of the Philippine Sea. A hit from a Yokosuka D4Y1 dive bomber killed 24 and wounded 27 men aboard battleship *South Dakota* on June 19, but the Japanese carriers *Taiho* and *Shokaku* were sunk by submarines *Albacore* and *Cavalla*, while carrier *Hiyo* was sunk by TBM-1s from light carrier *Belleau Wood* the next day. More important, the Japanese aircraft losses totaled 600, against 123 Americans.

Opposite: A marine on Saipan brings in Japanese prisoners on July 4, 1944. One member of the 2nd Marine Regiment, Private First Class Guy Gabaldon, a Mexican American from Los Angeles, California, who had learned Japanese from the Japanese American family with whom he had lived for some of his early years, managed to persuade some 1,500 Japanese soldiers and civilians to surrender on Saipan, for which he received the Navy Cross.

Left: Marines and a US Navy corpsman use a smokescreen to provide some concealment from Japanese attention as they rush a wounded marine to the rear on Saipan. While the marines advanced apace, Lieutenant General Holland M. Smith relieved Major General Ralph C. Smith of command for the comparatively slow progress of his 27th Infantry Division—failing to note that its troops had to negotiate more difficult cliffs and valleys than the marines against fanatical Japanese resistance.

"There is no longer any distinction between civilians and troops. It is better for them to join in the attack with bamboo spears than be captured."

—*Lieutenant General Yoshitsugu Saito, 43rd Division on Saipan.*

Above: American troops set up camouflaged tents as the fight for Saipan seems near its end. At that time, one enemy soldier surrendered to the author's father, navy combat cameraman Paul Guttman, while he was relieving himself outside camp. But in the morning of July 7, about 3,000 Japanese staged the war's largest banzai attack, ending with 650 American dead and wounded and 2,295 Japanese dead in the charge and 4,311 in total when the Americans retook lost ground 15 hours later.

Left: Nurses of the Women's Army Corps relax outside their quarters as the Americans settle in on Saipan and begin constructing the air bases from which B-29s will be able to carry out regular bombing strikes on Japan. Although officially banned from entering combat zones, many women did so and carried out their medical mission under fire—some even dying for their country when their facilities came under artillery or aerial bombing attack.

"Don't give them a damned inch!"

—Last words of Lieutenant Colonel William O'Brien, 1st Battalion, 105th Regiment, 27th Infantry Division, to his men facing the war's biggest banzai charge on Saipan, July 7, 1944. He was posthumously awarded the Medal of Honor.

Above: American troops examine the body and papers of a Japanese soldier killed in the July 7 banzai charge, after which Japanese troops and civilians began leaping to their deaths off Marpi Point. Of the 71,000 Americans who landed on Saipan, 2,949 were killed and 10,364 wounded. The 30,000 Japanese dead included General Saito and Vice Admiral Chuichi Nagumo, who had commanded the carrier attack on Pearl Harbor; both had committed ritual suicide in their caves on July 9.

Right: A Northrop P-61A-1 Black Widow in flight. Among the early units to receive the first night fighter designed from the ground up as such was the 6th Night Fighter Squadron on Saipan, which underwent nocturnal Japanese air raids throughout the war. On June 30, 1944, five days after its first operational flight, a P-61A crewed by Lieutenants Dale Haberman and Ray Mooney destroyed a G4M2 Betty over Saipan for the first of numerous Widow kills.

Below: *New Mexico*'s crew deploys a paravane, which was towed behind the ship to catch the mooring cables of tethered sea mines and bring them to the surface for disposal—usually by detonation. The crew is also using degaussing gear, which emitted electromagnetic signals to prematurely detonate magnetic mines. Although specialized minesweepers were used by both navies, all warships carried some equipment to deal with the omnipresent mine threat.

Left: Crewmen of the battleship *New Mexico* lower a 14-inch (35.5cm) shell into the ship's magazine in preparation for the liberation of Guam—which, aside from being the first American territory to be overrun by the Japanese, could provide airfields from which to bomb Japan. On July 14, one week before the scheduled landings, *New Mexico* was part of a force that gave the enemy defenses a preliminary pounding.

Right: Seen from a couple of US Navy destroyers, a Japanese plane, probably caught by a carrier fighter, makes its death plunge on July 10, 1944. In spite of the slaughter they underwent, lone Japanese reconnaissance "snoopers" and bombers, staging from Guam or the Bonin Islands, occasionally turned up over the Marianas. The Bonins, including Chichi Jima and Iwo Jima, were repeatedly raided by carrier task groups between June 15 and July 4.

Below: Battleship *New Mexico* returns to Guam on July 21, this time to support the landings of US Marines north and south of the Orote Peninsula. The battlewagon continued to use its 14-inch (35.5cm) guns to help the marines fend off a series of Japanese counterattacks until the two beachheads linked up on July 30. It then departed for Bremerton, Washington, to undergo an overhaul.

Left: The thinly armored Japanese Type 95 Ha-Go light tank, with its short 37mm gun, was pathetically outmatched on the Pacific islands on which it was deployed, but the one these marines are examining on Guam was a rare exception. In skillful cooperation with a second tank and an antitank gun, it helped destroy two M4 Sherman medium and two M5A1 Stuart light tanks before it was demolished.

Opposite: A Doberman and his handler, armed with a Thompson submachine gun, undergo jungle war training for Pacific service. The US Armed Forces trained 10,425 dogs in various military tasks, 9,300 of which served as sentries and 436 served overseas, where they proved invaluable in detecting the enemy's presence well in advance of their human partners. Eight of the 15 war dog platoons operated in the Pacific.

Left: A marine, armed with an M1 carbine, gets momentary rest on Guam. After holding off night infiltration attempts and banzai charges until July 30, and then fighting into the interior, the Americans declared the island secure on August 8. Some 18,040 Japanese were killed and 485 captured, but many held out for weeks, months, and even years thereafter; the last, Sergeant Shoichi Yokoi, was found in a cave on January 24, 1972.

Above: Marines look at a damaged temple on Tinian. Part of the Fifth Fleet shelled Tinian Town on the southwest side of the island as a feint, while 30,000 members of the 2nd and 4th Marine Divisions landed on the northwest tip on July 24, 1944. Tinian's terrain, less mountainous than Saipan's, favored American artillery and tank support, and marine F4U-1A Corsairs also made the first use of napalm there. The island was secured in four days.

Opposite bottom: Architects of the American Pacific offensive meet at Guam in August 1944; (from left) Major General Roy S. Geiger, commander of the III Marine Amphibious Corps, Admiral Raymond A. Spruance, commander of the Fifth Fleet, Lieutenant General Holland M. Smith, commanding ground forces in the Marianas, Admiral Chester W. Nimitz, commander in chief of the Pacific Fleet, and Lieutenant General Alexander A. Vandegrift, Commandant of the Marine Corps and Medal of Honor recipient during the Battle of Guadalcanal.

Above: Vincent Salvaggo and John D. Snowell tend to a Doberman pinscher on Guam. Typifying the specially trained canines' contribution throughout the Pacific, dogs of the 2nd and 3rd War Dog Platoons, capable of detecting the enemy at 1,000 feet (305m), walked at the head of 550 patrols on Guam, their timely warnings preventing ambushes in each case. Nevertheless, 26 dogs were killed in the Marianas, along with three of their handlers killed on Guam and four on Saipan.

Japanese POWs

The failure of the Japanese to sign the 1929 Geneva Accords and their insistence on treating prisoners by the same harsh Bushido code by which they fought—which regarded surrender as an act of profound dishonor—combined with mutual racism to make neither the Japanese nor the Allies willing to either become a prisoner or to take an enemy alive in the Pacific War's early years. As the Allied offensive progressed, however, they established camps that treated Japanese POWs according to Geneva rules.

In spite of the Japanese government's attempt to reinforce Bushido with propaganda that the Allies would torture and kill them if they surrendered, growing numbers of weary, disillusioned Japanese preferred captivity to death. Since doing so completely cut them off from home, the POWs were usually cooperative, providing intelligence and even suggestions for persuading more of their comrades to give themselves up. By the end of the war, 42,543 Japanese were recorded as surrendering to the Americans and Australians, with another estimated 35,000 surrendering to the British or Chinese in Asia.

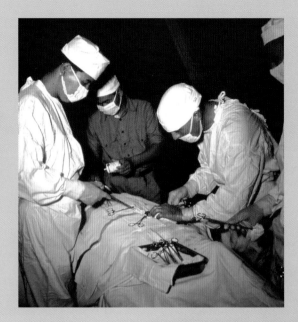

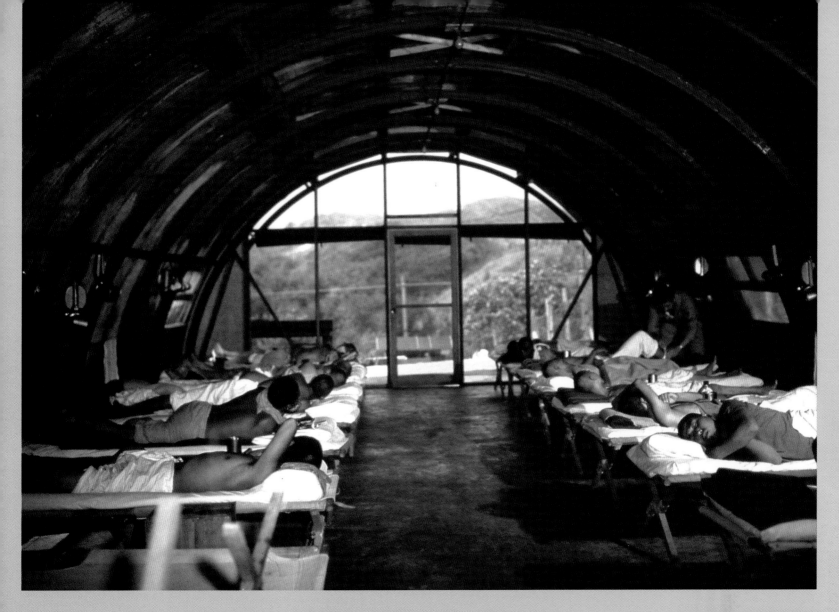

Above: Injured and sick Japanese POWs rest in a quonset hut infirmary in the Guam stockade.

Opposite top: A US Navy surgeon and Japanese assistants, one of whom (in center) administers ether, operate on a POW in the Guam stockade.

Opposite: Japanese prisoners, all in their original issue uniforms in various states of wear, receive instructions from an American at a POW stockade on Guam.

Right: POWs organize a baseball game at the Guam stockade. Japan had enthusiastically embraced the American game of baseball long before the war, and would send stars of its own to the American major leagues in the postwar years.

Opposite top: Members of a US Navy construction battalion lay a four-lane highway on Guam. Forming shortly after the attack on Pearl Harbor, the CBs, or Seabees, were generally made up of volunteers with a variety of civilian skills. Provided with additional combat training by the marines, the Seabees built the installations that followed American progress toward Japan, as well as detaching Underwater Demolition Teams to clear beaches of mines and other obstacles ahead of the marines—precursors of the modern Navy SEALs.

Left: Shipfitter Second Class Steven J. Kusial pauses from his labors on the Seabee road crew on Guam for the photographer. The author's father, then 23-year-old Paul Guttman, began as a camouflage expert with the 59th CB whose members called him "Kid" since the average Seabee's age was 37 and a few were in their 60s. For comparison, members of a nearby marine regiment, most aged 20 or younger, referred to Guttman as "Pops."

Opposite: Tinian-based Boeing B-29 42-24797 *Jackpot* of the 505th Bomb Group, which had been partially sponsored by members of the 107th Construction Battalion, gets an added dedication in the form of the CB mascot, "Joe Seabee"; (from left) Painter First Class Edmund D Wright, Corporal Marion V. Lewis, and Sergeant Frank E. Schleicher. Photographed on March 7, 1945, *Jackpot* ditched 150 miles (241km) off Japan due to flak damage 12 days later.

Boosting Morale

World War II in the Pacific entailed an unprecedented number of service personnel serving farther from home in more remote locations than any had known outside of the British Empire. Given the added isolation involved, opportunities for rest and recreation were arguably of greater importance to the fighting forces there than in the European theater.

For Allied troops in the South Pacific, leave to Australia offered the readiest break—and in the process solidified Australian-American rapport that had been close since their troops had operated together in World War I. An extraordinary Japanese measure for troop morale was to send "comfort girls," in essence, government-sponsored prostitutes, to the battlefronts. Although the troops often sang their praises, it was revealed postwar that thousands of them were not volunteers, but Koreans and other captives of the "Co-Prosperity Sphere" forced into such service against their will.

In 1941 President Roosevelt called for a mobilization of resources for troop morale, leading to the formation of the privately funded but Department of Defense-supported United Service Organizations, encompassing the Salvation Army, Young Men's Christian Association, Young Women's Christian Organization, National Catholic Community Service, National Travel Aid Association, and National Jewish Welfare Board. By the end of the war, 1.5 million Americans were serving in the USO in one capacity or other.

Above: Terry Perez practices between acts with a stage troupe organized by Seabee Chaplain Harold F. Menges to entertain servicemen on or visiting Guam with native songs and dances.

Above right: Hollywood became heavily involved in USO activities with camp shows and the "Stage Door Canteen," but the most ubiquitous presence overseas was Bob Hope and his traveling troupe, which performed everywhere from Casablanca to Okinawa.

Opposite: A girl serves cake to a sailor at a USO hospitality house in Astoria, Oregon. Hospitality houses were a "home away from home" to service personnel in transit to their actual destinations.

Right: Sailors look over the activities list at a Fleet Recreation Center in Purvis Bay, Florida Island, near Guadalcanal, on April 21, 1944.

Left: A North American P-51C Mustang, bearing the famous Flying Tiger shark mouth of the 23rd Fighter Group, sits ready for the next mission from Kweilin in mid-1944. In 1943 the Fourteenth Air Force received its first Allison-engine P-51As, which it operated until the first Rolls-Royce Merlin engine P-51Bs and P-51Cs arrived. Gradually eclipsing the aging P-40s, the Mustangs allowed the Fourteenth Air Force to maintain its edge over the best Japanese fighters arriving in 1944, including the Nakajima Ki.84 *Hayate* ("Gale").

> "I predict that the Fourteenth will still be operating in China when the last Jap on Chinese soil has passed through the gates of a prisoner of war camp."
>
> —*Major General Clarie L. Chennault, responding to news articles describing the Fourteenth Air Force's position as precarious.*

Left: *Lonesome Polecat, Jr.,* A B-24J-80-CO of the 425th Squadron, 308th Bomb Group (Heavy), undergoes maintenance between missions for the Fourteenth Air Force. First joining the Fourteenth Air Force by flying the Hump loaded with all the supplies its B-24Ds could carry, the 308th Group carried out raids to Japanese air bases and seaports as far as the Chinese coast, Southeast Asia, and the South China Sea.

Above: A camouflaged Boeing B-29 of the XX Bomber Command arrives in China as part of Operation Matterhorn, a bombing campaign from Chinese bases. The first strike, against Bangkok, Thailand, took place on June 5, 1944, and on June 15 the B-29s attacked Yawada, the first bombing of the home islands since the Doolittle raid of April 18, 1942. Operations continued until March 1945, when the last contingent, the 58th Bomber Wing, joined the rest of XX Bomber Command in the Marianas.

Left: Major General Albert C. Wedemeyer chats with Generalissimo Chiang Kai-shek. After General George C. Marshall notified him on October 27, 1944, that he was replacing General Joseph Stilwell as Chiang's chief of staff, Wedemeyer arrived to find that Stilwell had departed, leaving him no information on how to deal with the Chinese leader. Wedemeyer sought to persuade Chiang to use his army more aggressively while coordinating the Fourteenth and Twentieth Air Forces' efforts in China.

Douglas MacArthur (1880–1964)

The son of Civil War Medal of Honor recipient Arthur MacArthur Jr., Douglas MacArthur also pursued a US Army career, being awarded the Distinguished Service Cross for his actions in the Veracruz landing in 1914 and as chief of staff for the 42nd "Rainbow" Division in 1914. After World War I he served in the Philippines, returned to West Point as superintendent, was then US Army chief of staff, and finally took command of US forces in the Philippines. As the Japanese overran the islands, MacArthur and his family departed Corregidor in a PT boat in March 1942. Awarded the Medal of Honor for his efforts there—the only case of father and son receiving the medal—MacArthur became Supreme Commander, Southwest Pacific Area, and embarked on an offensive aimed at fulfilling a promise he had made before leaving the Philippines: "I shall return."

Opposite top: An LCD (landing ship, dock) crowded with smaller landing craft approaches Morotai on September 14, 1944. The 31st Infantry Division came ashore in the face of light opposition the next day, and by the twenty-fourth it had secured a sufficient perimeter for an airfield and a PT boat base to be established. Morotai was intended to serve as a jumping-off point for MacArthur's invasion of Mindanao in the Philippines, scheduled for November 15.

Above: The captain of an LST (landing ship, tank) lying off the coast of Morotai checks his navigational bearings. In addition to two air bases, Morotai supplied PT boat bases and a jumping off point for the invasion of Borneo.

Opposite: Crewmen of a battleship's 40mm and 20mm antiaircraft guns take a breather off Peleliu on September 15, 1944. The 1st Marine Division lost 200 dead and 900 wounded in the hotly contested landings, but the Marines, with air, armor, and warship support, secured the beachhead and wiped out a light tank-backed counterattack. The airfield was taken the next day, seeming to confirm Major General William H. Rupertus's assertion that Peleliu would be secured within four days.

"Our sword
is broken and
we have run out
of spears."

*—Last report from
Colonel Kunio Nakagawa,
2nd Regiment, 14th Infantry
Division, from Peleliu before
he burned his regimental colors
and committed ritual suicide
on November 25, 1944.
For his stubborn defense of
Peleliu, the Japanese army
posthumously promoted him
to lieutenant general.*

Right: Members of the 1st Marine Division examine a captured Japanese 37mm cannon on Peleliu. Contrary to American expectations that resistance would crumble soon after the landings, Japanese Colonel Kunio Nakagawa used some 500 limestone caves in the Umubrogol Mountains to conduct a murderous in-depth defense until November 27. By then the strategic importance of the island, which cost 1,794 American and 10,695 Japanese lives, had been mooted by the American landings in the Philippines.

Below: Consolidated B-24J Liberators of the 320th Squadron, 90th Bomb Group fly a long-range mission over the southwestern Pacific. The securing of Noemfoor Island on July 7, and Morotai on September 15, brought the Far East Air Forces to 2,600 miles (4,184km) of the Japanese-held oil refineries at Balikpapan, Borneo. On September 30 and October 3, 10, 14 and 18, B-24s dropped 433 tons (390 tonnes) of bombs to cripple the facilities for the rest of 1944.

David McCampbell (1910–1996)

Born in Bessemer, Alabama, David McCampbell, here portrayed by carrier *Essex* photographer Jack Stewart in his F6F-5 *Minsi III* as commander of Air Group 15, graduated from the US Naval Academy in 1933 and obtained his "Wings of Gold" in 1938. During the Battle of the Philippine Sea, McCampbell shot down seven Japanese planes on June 19, 1944. On October 24, he set an American one-mission record of nine enemy planes destroyed over the Sibuyan Sea; his wingman, Lieutenant Junior Grade Roy W. Rushing, got another six. Awarded the Medal of Honor, McCampbell scored his thirty-fourth victory on November 14, making him the US Navy's ace of aces. Retiring from the navy in 1964, he died in 1996.

Above: (from left) Lieutenant General George Kenney (in the background), Lieutenant General Richard Sutherland, Philippine President Sergio Osmena, General MacArthur, and Brigadier General Carlos Romula (with head turned toward MacArthur) ride a landing craft toward Leyte on October 20, 1944. The beginning of the fulfillment of MacArthur's promised return to the Philippines also brought on an attempt by the Japanese navy to annihilate the beachhead in the Battle of Leyte Gulf on October 24 and 25.

Opposite: Curtiss SB2C-4 Helldiver crew in 1944. Initially despised as the "Son-of-a-Bitch 2nd Class," the overweight, underpowered SB2C-1 was replaced by the SB2C-3, whose many improvements included a 1,900hp engine (compared to the SB2C-1's 1,700hp). At Leyte Gulf, Helldivers helped sink the battleship *Musashi* in the Sibuyan Sea on October 24 and four Japanese aircraft carriers off Cape Engaño the next day. Ultimately, 7,140 were built, making the Helldiver history's most-produced dive bomber.

August–October 1944 *Romania dismisses pro-Axis Prime Minister Ion Antonescu and goes over to the Allies on August 23. A Polish uprising in Warsaw and a Slovak uprising centered around Tri Duby are ultimately crushed by the Germans.*

September 17–25, 1944 *Operation Market-Garden, an Allied airborne-ground combined operation to liberate the Netherlands, is defeated at Arnhem and ends in failure as German forces counterattack.*

December 16, 1944 *Germans launch a major offensive into the Ardennes Forest, culminating in the Battle of the Bulge, in which the Germans are fatally delayed at Trois-Ponts and Bastogne, and flanked by General George Patton's Third Army.*

December 26, 1944 *Soviet and Romanian armies encircle Budapest, beginning the war's most intense and destructive siege of a European city after Leningrad and Warsaw.*

"What man can say that there is no chance for our fleet to turn the tide of war in a decisive battle? You must all remember there are such things as miracles."

—*Vice Admiral Takeo Kurita before the Battle of Leyte Gulf, in which he turned away just short of reaching the American beachhead on October 25, 1944.*

Left: An SB2C-3 Helldiver prepares for takeoff from a *Casablanca*-class escort carrier. Six such ships made up Task Unit 77.4.3, or "Taffy 3," when it came under attack from Vice Admiral Takeo Kurita's battle force, but between its own planes and those of nearby Taffies 1 and 2, some 400 were available to harass the Japanese warships. Although enemy cruisers caught and sank the escort carrier *Gambier Bay*, one of its victorious assailants, *Chikuma*, was sunk shortly afterward by air attacks.

Above: A newly liberated Tacloban and its airfield face the island of Samar, scene of the Battle of Leyte Gulf's critical phase. On October 25, Kurita's battle fleet arrived off Samar, opposed only by two escort carrier task units and aircraft operating from Tacloban. In the fighting retreat that ensued, the escorts convinced Kurita to retire, saving the Leyte beachhead, sinking three Japanese heavy cruisers but losing two escort carriers, two destroyers, and a destroyer escort.

John S. McCain (1884–1945)

Born in Carroll County, Mississippi, John Sidney McCain graduated from the US Naval Academy in 1906, a lackluster 79th in a class of 116. He was Commander Air South Pacific in the critical months of May through October 1942, subsequently heading the Bureau of Aeronautics and leading Task Group 38.1 before taking command of Task Force 38 on October 30, 1944. On December 18, McCain was involved in Admiral Bill Halsey's disastrous decision to remain on station in the South China Sea in the face of a massive typhoon that mauled the Third Fleet and sank three destroyers. McCain departed on January 26, 1945, but reassumed command of Task Force 38 on May 28. Worn out and down to 100 pounds (45.5kg), McCain delayed his homecoming long enough to take part in Japan's surrender, but died four days later on September 6, 1945.

Opposite: The rangefinder aboard an escort carrier was normally for zeroing in on enemy aircraft, but during the Battle of Samar six shells from *White Plains'* aft-mounted 5-inch (12.5cm) gun struck the heavy cruiser *Chokai*, blowing up its torpedo tubes and compelling the Japanese to abandon it and leave it to sink. Less fortunate were *Gambier Bay*, sunk by Japanese cruisers and *St. Lô*, which shortly after became the first warship sunk by a kamikaze.

Right: A young Leyte resident salutes an officer of the 345th Bomb Group at Dulag, where the unit arrived and commenced Philippine operations on October 28. Equipped with B-25Hs and B-25Js, the 345th, known as the "Air Apaches," had developed a specialty in low-level strafing against land and sea targets alike from New Guinea to Ie Shima, receiving the US Distinguished Unit Citation and the Philippine Presidential Unit Citation.

Hiroyoshi Nishizawa (1920–1944)

Japan produced a number of outstanding exponents of the Mitsubishi A6M Zero, but its leading ace, Hiroyoshi Nishizawa, attained mythic status as "The Devil." A natural pilot, credited with 87 victories, including six over Guadalcanal on August 7, 1942, he survived the attrition that whittled away so many of his comrades over the Solomons. His last two victories were over F6F Hellcats while escorting the first kamikazes off Samar on October 25, 1944. The next day, the ace who was reputedly invincible in the cockpit of his Zero was shot down and killed by Lieutenant Junior Grade Harold P. Newell of carrier *Wasp*'s VF-14—while riding a transport plane from Mabalacat to Clark Field.

Below: Ordered to depart Manila for Brunei carrying Vice Admiral Kiyohide Shima aboard, the light cruiser *Kiso*—which had evacuated 1,189 troops from Kiska Island under the Allies' noses on July 28, 1943—was just getting underway on November 13, when it was attacked by carrier planes from Task Groups 38.1, 38.3 and 38.4. Struck by three bombs, the vessel sank in the shallows eight miles (13km) west of Cavite, although most of its crew survived. *Kiso*'s remains were salvaged on December 15, 1955.

Left: A Kawanishi N1K1-J *Shiden* ("Violet Lightning") of *Hikotai* (squadron) 402, 341st Kokutai lies abandoned on Clark Field's Mabalacat airstrip, where most of the unit's fighters were destroyed on the ground by the end of November 1944. Developed from the N1K1 floatplane fighter, the midwing *Shiden* mounted four 20mm cannons, but its complex landing gear and middling performance led to a simplified version with lowered wings, the superb N1K2-J *Shiden-Kai*. Both variants were given the Allied codename "George."

Richard Ira Bong (1920–1945)

Returning to the Fifth Air Force as a gunnery officer in V Fighter Command—in essence, a roving commission—Major Richard Bong downed two Japanese fighters while accompanying a bombing raid to Balikpapan on October 10, 1944. Operating from Tacloban airfield over the Philippines, he swiftly brought his tally to 37, and on December 13 General MacArthur awarded him the Medal of Honor. On the seventeenth, Bong scored his fortieth victory, and General Kenney sent him home for the last time. Tragically, the American ace of aces was killed while test flying a Lockheed P-80 jet fighter on August 6, 1945.

Above: Crewmen clean up the port 5-inch (12.5cm) gun battery aboard the light cruiser *Nashville* (CL-43) after a kamikaze hit on December 13, 1944, while the 24th Infantry Division's 19th Regiment and the 503rd Parachute Regimental Combat Team land on Mindoro. The island and its air base were secured on the sixteenth, but Japanese army suicide planes damaged *Nashville*, killing 130 crewmen and wounding 190—including the landing force commander, Brigadier General William C. Dunkel—and two LSTs.

Chapter 5

Blood and Fire

Closing in on the home islands

The New Year began throughout the world with the Allies on the advance and the Axis indulging in acts of desperation. Germany expended its forces in a final series of offensives—Operations Bodenplatte and Nordwind in the west, Operations Konrad and Spring Awakening in the east, all only serving to hasten the inevitable. In Asia the British were on the road to Mandalay, and their fleet was striking its way back into the eastern Indian Ocean. On Luzon, General Douglas MacArthur's forces liberated Manila and moved on other islands throughout the Philippines. From the Marianas, B-29 Superfortresses were bombing and burning Japan's cities to the ground. Only in China was the Japanese army still striving to maintain the offensive, though its prospects of sustaining such an effort were fast becoming moot.

In the western Pacific, US Navy carriers struck at will at targets in Indochina, Formosa, and Japan itself, while targeting two key islands as the last stepping stones on the road to Tokyo. The first, Iwo Jima, offered an airfield where damaged B-29s could find sanctuary short of the Marianas, and from which long-range fighters could escort the bombers. Further along, Okinawa would be the final staging base for the invasion of Japan itself.

First, however, those islands would have to be taken, and the commanders assigned to defend them were determined to make the Americans pay for them in both time and blood. On Iwo, Lieutenant General Tadamichi Kobayashi had prepared a comprehensive network of underground defenses. On Okinawa, Lieutenant General Mitsuru Ushijima also planned a slow, stubborn fighting retreat, while the supporting US Navy would be eliminated by waves of suicidal kamikaze pilots crashing their planes into the enemy's ships. With these two battles, World War II's last act would be a fiery climax indeed.

Above: A marine in the Russell Islands prepares grave markers early in 1945 in order to provide the next invasion force a ready supply if necessary. Although the Japanese had been suffering defeats on every front except China throughout 1944, their continued determination to fight to the death, demonstrated on every island and strongpoint they defended that year, gave the Allies good reason to anticipate heavy casualties as they closed in on the home islands.

Right: A crewman works at the control board of the carrier Yorktown's damage control room. Damage control precautions and procedures, developed from bitter lessons learned in 1942, manifested themselves, among other things, in comparing the four fleet carriers the US Navy lost in 1942 to its only such loss in 1944, the light carrier Princeton at Leyte Gulf. Japanese suicide planes, however, would test the damage control crews as never before in 1945.

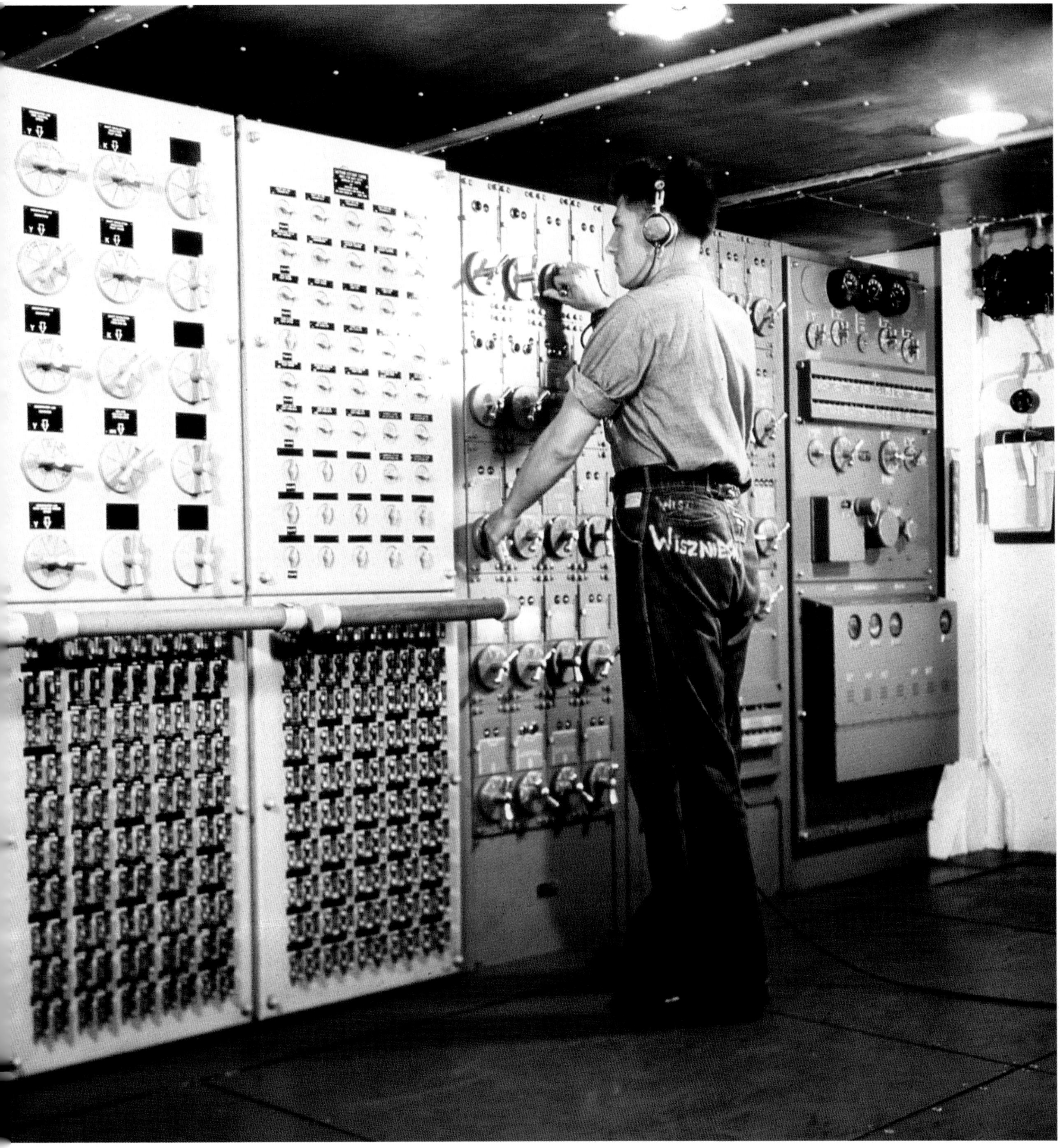

January 1, 1945 *In Operation Bodenplatte, Luftwaffe fighters strike at Allied airfields, but suffer irreplaceable losses. Heinrich Himmler launches Operation Nordwind against the US Seventh Army, only to be halted at Strasbourg.*

January 1, 7, 17 and 20, 1945 *German Operations Konrad I, II and III, and a final southern offensive, try to retake Budapest and the Danube River, coming within 12.5 miles (20km) before failing. Budapest surrenders on February 13.*

"They said the job of building this road could not be done. But thousands of American engineers, Chinese engineers, and soldiers proved that it could. There stands the proof!"

—*Brigadier General Lewis A. Pick upon arrival in Kunming via the Ledo Road, February 4, 1945.*

Above: Brigadier General Lewis A. Pick addresses the Chinese in Kunming on February 4, 1945, 23 days after his 113-truck convoy departed Ledo, Assam, along the newly completed Ledo Road. Begun in December 1942 by General Joseph Stilwell after the Japanese overran the Burma Road, the 1,075-mile-long (1,736km) Ledo Road—later renamed the Stilwell Road—was carved through mountains as high as 4,500 feet (1,400m), allowing trucks to bring 129,000 tons (117,027 tonnes) of supplies to China over the following six months.

Right: Assigned to General Douglas MacArthur as his British military representative in 1943, Lieutenant General Herbert Lumsden, here conferring with a US Army officer in the Solomons, was aboard the battleship *New Mexico* in Lingayen Gulf off Luzon on January 6, 1945, when a Japanese suicide plane struck the bridge, killing him. Kamikazes sank 24 US Navy ships and damaged 67 others in Lingayen Gulf between January 4 and 12.

April 25, 1945 *Soviets encircle Berlin; General George S. Patton's Third Army crosses the Danube at Regensburg; Soviet and US troops meet at the Elbe River near Torgau; conference begins in San Francisco on a United Nations Constitution.*

April 28, 1945 *Benito Mussolini, his mistress, Clara Petacci, and most of his 15-person entourage of Repubblica Sociale Italiana officials are shot by communist partisans in Giulino di Mezzegra.*

Above: Flag and beach markers signify that the American beachhead in Lingayen Gulf has been secured. On January 9, 1945, 68,000 troops of Lieutenant General Walter Krueger's Sixth Army, together with the Philippine troops, came ashore in the face of virtually no resistance and swiftly liberated the port of Dagupan, along with the adjacent cities of Lingayen, Binmaley, and San Fabian.

Left: Philippine Commonwealth soldiers join their American liberators in a parade through the streets of Dagupan on January 9. By the twelfth, more than 208,000 US Army troops were on Luzon and began moving south in a race to liberate the Philippine capital city of Manila as well as prisoner of war camps, such as Cabanatuan, before the Japanese could murder the inmates.

The Bloody Liberation of Manila

Although organized resistance on Luzon officially ended on June 9, 1942, as the Japanese advanced through the rest of the Philippines, they encountered continual resistance from Filipino guerrilla groups. The "death marches" that American and Filipino prisoners of war underwent, en route to years of brutal treatment in POW camps, represented a distillation of Japan's harsh rule over the Philippines in general.

The landings in Lingayen Gulf in January 1945 were the prelude toward the liberation of Luzon and the Philippine capital of Manila, but it would prove to be an event more akin to the horrors of Warsaw and Budapest than the triumph of Paris. Judging the city indefensible, General Tomoyuki

Yamashita chose to evacuate his Fourteenth Area Army and conduct a fighting retreat in the forests and mountains outside the city. However, a fanatical naval officer, Rear Admiral Sanji Iwabuchi, ignored Yamashita's evacuation order and organized the 10,000 naval and 4,000 army personnel who remained behind for his stated goal of turning Manila into a "Pacific Stalingrad."

On February 3, the US 1st Cavalry Division overran Santo Tomás internment camp, liberating 5,785 prisoners. From then on, however, it took a month of house-to-house fighting to liberate the capital, at a cost of 1,010 American, 12,000 Japanese, and about 100,000 Filipino civilian lives.

Opposite bottom: The remains of Manila's Intramuros on April 22. Fighting for the walled complex began on February 23 and lasted five days. The last pocket of Japanese resistance was overcome in the Finance Building on March 3.

Below: A building on the Escorita lies demolished after the Battle of Manila.

Right: Private Charles P. Cooper holds a sniper version of the M-1 Garand rifle with telescopic sight and muzzle flash hider. The weapon was used by specialists within units such as the 6th Ranger Battalion, which, together with Filipino guerrillas, forged ahead of the Sixth Army to raid Cabanatuan on January 30, liberating 522 prisoners and killing or wounding 525 Japanese for the loss of two Rangers killed, four wounded, and 20 Filipinos wounded.

Tomoyuki Yamashita (1885–1946)

The son of a doctor, Tomoyuki Yamashita graduated from the Imperial Japanese Army Academy in 1906 and fought the Germans in Shantung, China, in 1914. An opponent of Hideki Tojo, he advocated Japanese withdrawal from China and the maintenance of peaceful relations with Britain and the United States until Japan committed itself to war. As commander of the Twenty-Fifth Army, Yamashita led his 30,000 troops in a brilliant campaign through Malaya to take Singapore and 130,000 prisoners on February 15, 1942, a humiliating blow to the British Empire that earned him the sobriquet of "Tiger of Malaya." His continuing friction with Tojo got him sidelined in Manchukuo until October 10, 1944, when he was put in command of the Fourteenth Area Army on Luzon. There he used his 152,000 troops to conduct a protracted fighting retreat until September 2, 1945, when he surrendered his 50,000 remaining men. The first Japanese leader to be tried as a war criminal, for atrocities committed by men under his command at Singapore and Manila—although he had left the latter and had had no contact with those Japanese who stayed behind to fight there—Yamashita was convicted after a trial that was both controversial and precedent-setting, and was hanged at Los Baños on February 23, 1946.

> "The Accused is not charged with having done something or having failed to do something, but solely with having been something."
>
> —Colonel Harry E. Clarke, chief counsel for the defense at General Tomoyuki Yamashita's war crimes trial.

Opposite: After its commissioning on September 26, 1944, LST-942 (landing ship, tank) sets out for the Visaya Islands in the Philippines. The Visayas campaign began on March 19, 1945, when the 40th Infantry Division of Lieutenant General Robert L. Eichelberger's Eighth Army landed on Panay. Aided by Filipino guerrillas, over the next two months the Eighth Army swiftly moved on to liberate that objective, followed by the islands of Guimaras, Inampulagan, Cebu, Negros, and Bohol.

Left: A crewman adds railroad boxcars to PT-134's scoreboard after a raid on Japanese transport facilities in Cebu City on March 24, 1945. On the twenty-sixth, the Americal Division landed at Talisay Beach and marched into Cebu City the next day. Although Lieutenant General Takeo Manjome's 102nd Division fought on, 2,000 of his 14,500 men were tied down by 8,500 Filipino guerrillas in the north.

Below: A wounded soldier air evacuated from the Philippines gets a drink of water from a corpsman under the wing of the Consolidated PB4Y-3 flying boat that flew him out. With the Americans outflanking him, on April 16 General Manjome withdrew his 8,500 surviving troops into northern Cebu, where they remained for the rest of the war. After May 28, fighting in the Visayas was primarily limited to mopping-up operations by the Filipino guerrillas.

Robert L. Eichelberger (1886–1961)

Born in Urbana, Ohio, Robert Lawrence Eichelberger graduated 68 out of 103 in the class of 1909 at the US Military Academy at West Point, alongside George S. Patton Jr. (46th) and Jacob Devers (39th). He served thereafter in Panama, the US-Mexican border, and in the American Expeditionary Force in Siberia in 1919, during which he was awarded the Distinguished Service Cross and three Japanese decorations—and was able to observe the Japanese army in action. From 1940 to 1942 he served as superintendent at West Point, where he is shown in the photograph. At a time when many American officers wanted to affix their Japanese medals to bombs, Eichelberger demurred, declaring, "Hell, no, I'm going to take them back myself."

As commander of the I Corps in 1942, Eichelberger was privately disliked by troops of the 32nd Infantry Division for the "Prussian" discipline he enforced, but he led from the front, and under his command the Australian-American forces took Buna, followed by further successes at Hollandia and Biak. As commander of the Eighth Army, Eichelberger conducted a series of swift campaigns to liberate the Philippine islands of Mindoro, Marinduque, Panay, Negros, Cebu, Bohol, and Mindanao by July 1945. In August, he and the Eighth Army began a three-year occupation of Japan. Denied a Medal of Honor at General Douglas MacArthur's insistence, Eichelberger retired in September 1948, but received an honorary promotion to full general in 1954.

> "... the model of what a light but aggressive campaign can accomplish in rapid exploitation."
>
> ——*General Douglas MacArthur praising Lieutenant General Robert L. Eichelberger's conduct of the Visayas campaign.*

Right: A deck handling party gets some sun on a Hellcat's ample wing aboard a British carrier on January 18, 1945. After stopping at Trincomalee, Ceylon, Task Force 63, commanded by Rear Admiral Philip L. Vian and centered on carriers *Indomitable, Illustrious, Indefatigable*, and *Victorious*, departed for Fremantle, Australia, on January 13. Along the way, it was to strike at the oil refineries at Palembang, Sumatra.

Right: Aircrewmen wheel a 21-inch (53cm) torpedo to a Grumman Avenger in Ceylon in early 1945. For some six months, Avengers of numbers 832 and 845 squadrons operated from Ceylon and from the escort carriers *Begum* and *Shah*. While aboard the latter, they participated in an eight-day hunt for a German submarine in the Indian Ocean that ended on August 12, 1944, when British frigate *Findhorn* and Indian sloop *Godavari* depth charged and sank *U-198* with all 66 hands.

Louis Mountbatten, 1st Earl Mountbatten of Burma (1900–1979)

Admiral Lord Louis Mountbatten, shown driving a jeep on Ceylon in November 1944, was born Prince Louis of Battenberg, later having his name anglicized. He served as a midshipman in World War I, and in World War II he distinguished himself as captain of the destroyer *Kelly* until it was dive-bombed and sunk off Crete on May 23, 1941. In October 1943 Mountbatten was made Supreme Allied Commander South East Asia Command, in which capacity he displayed considerable diplomatic talents in dealing with Joseph Stilwell and Chiang Kai-shek. On September 12, 1945, Mountbatten accepted Japanese General Seishiro Itagaki's surrender at Singapore. As the last viceroy of India, Mountbatten presided over the independence of India and Pakistan on August 14–15, 1947, and subsequently served as First Sea Lord. On August 27, 1979, Lord Mountbatten and four others were killed near Mullaghmore, Ireland, by a bomb planted on his fishing boat, *Shadow V*, by Thomas McMahon of the Provisional Irish Republican Army.

The Palembang Raids

Since its fall on February 15, 1942, the Palembang oil fields in Sumatra had produced 50 percent of Japan's oil and 75 percent of its aviation fuel. On January 4, 1945, Rear Admiral Philip L. Vian's Task Force 63, including the aircraft carriers *Victorious*, *Indomitable*, and *Indefatigable*, marked the Royal Navy's return to the Pacific in force by launching a 90-plane strike on the oil refinery at Pangkalan Brandan.

To attack the objective, the British planes would have to approach it over a 7,000-foot (2km) mountain range and then run a gauntlet of antiaircraft guns, barrage balloons, and Japanese army fighters. Later that month the British returned, and after a three-day delay due to bad weather, on the morning of January 24, 43 Avengers bombed the Plajoe oil refineries north of Palembang, during which 12 Fairey Firefly fighter-bombers of *Indefatigable*'s No. 1770 Squadron first used their 60-pound (27kg) underwing rockets against enemy targets. Extensive damage was done, but 32 planes were shot down or written off in crash landings. On January 29 the carrier planes returned to Palembang for Operation Meridian II, this time bombing the Soengei Gerong refineries. The British lost 16 planes in Meridian II, but claimed a total of 37 Japanese planes destroyed in the air and 38 on the ground. More important, though, they had substantially reduced Palembang's output, some of its facilities being out of commission for the rest of the war.

Above: A pilot poses beside his Hellcat before the strike on Palembang.

Left: Deck crewmen prepare to load 500-pound (227kg) bombs into an Avenger's torpedo bay for Operation Meridian I, the Palembang raid.

Opposite: Hellcats prepare to take off from *Indomitable* in January 1945. Besides escorting the Avengers through scores of Japanese fighters, one Hellcat joined the Seafires that defended the carriers from a counterattack by seven Mitsubishi Ki.21 bombers and Ki.46 reconnaissance planes.

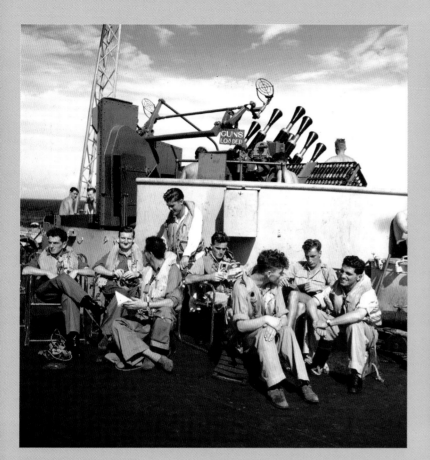

Above: A Grumman Hellcat pilot sits on standby alert aboard a British aircraft carrier off the coast of Sumatra.

Above left: British pilots wait for orders for the next strike in front of their carrier's pom-pom guns in January 1945.

> "Our enemies could always be relied on to retaliate and this was no exception and a fairly substantial one too."
>
> —Michael J. H. Davey, a Supermarine Seafire pilot of No. 894 Squadron, HMS Indefatigable.

Right: *Havildar* (Sergeant) Kulbahadur Gurung of the 2nd (King Edward VII's Own) Gurkha Regiment in Burma brandishes a Sten gun in February 1945. During fighting near Tamandu on March 5, 1945, *Havildar* Bhanbhagta Gurung of the 2nd Gurkhas exposed himself in order to pick off a Japanese sniper, then advanced alone to eliminate four Japanese defensive positions with rifle, grenades, and bayonet. After that, he killed the three occupants of a bunker with his kukri. He was awarded the Victoria Cross.

Opposite: Royal Marine commandos train with a portable radio telephone set on Ceylon in January 1945. Following their occupation of Akyab Island on December 31, 1944, the British began advancing along the southern coast of Burma. On January 12, 1945, the 42nd (Royal Marine) Commando landed on the Myebon Peninsula to start a pincer movement with British forces to the north. The taking of Kangaw on January 29 drove scattered Japanese remnants from the peninsula.

Opposite bottom: A Royal Marine reconnaissance patrol trains on crossing a river by native canoe in January 1945, in preparation for the taking of Cheduba Island off the Burmese coast. On January 21 the British landed on Cheduba, only to discover there was no Japanese garrison, and on Ramree Island, whose garrison stubbornly resisted the Royal Marines for six weeks until the Japanese finally evacuated what remained of their troops.

Right: Troops of the 19th Indian Division raise the Union Flag at Fort Dufferin, as the British called the old fortress, whose walls and moats allowed the Japanese 15th Division to repulse several attempts to storm it, including one attempt to sneak in through the fort's sewer system. Finally, on the twentieth, General Yamamoto managed to convince his commanders that further resistance would be a waste of manpower, and the remaining Japanese troops slipped out through the sewer system.

Above: British troops rest between assaults in Mandalay in March 1945. On March 3 the British took Meiktila, and on the eighth the 19th Indian Division moved on Mandalay. Lieutenant General Seiei Yamamoto, reporting his 15th Division to be seriously understrength, opposed defending the city, but his superior, Lieutenant General Hyotaro Kimura, insisted upon a defense to the death rather than lose the center of communication in Burma and the ammunition stockpiles south of Mandalay.

Right: British troops pause before one of the many Buddhas on Mandalay's Pagoda Hill. In April, General Slim's forces resumed their advance down the Irrawaddy River in a bid to liberate Rangoon before the monsoon season. On May 1, Operation Dracula began as Gurkha paratroops secured Elephant Point on the Rangoon River, followed by an amphibious landing by the 26th Indian Division the next day—to find Rangoon abandoned. Monsoon rains began just hours later.

Below: British troops stand to as the Union Flag is ceremoniously re-raised over Fort Dufferin. Among other consequences, revolts broke out in the Japanese-sponsored Burmese National Army, which joined Burmese guerrillas in turning on the Japanese. After trying to retake Meiktila from March 5 through 28, the Japanese, seeing their supply and communication lines cut, began a poorly organized withdrawal eastward through Burma.

Opposite: A crewman poses before *Wabash Cannonball*, a North American B-25H-1 of the 491st "Ringer" Squadron, 341st Bomb Group, which flew 40 missions in the Yankai Valley throughout 1944 and 1945. Armed with a 75mm cannon, the B-25H was extensively used by the Tenth Air Force for "bridge-busting" as well as for tactical bombing and strafing in the China-Burma-India theater of operations.

Above: Marine Corporal Osbourne Cheek and Sergeant George W. Ewell scan the horizon atop a 5-inch (12.7cm)/38 caliber gun mount on the "large cruiser" Alaska during a firing exercise in February 1945. Alaska and its sister ship Guam were essentially battle cruisers, with a main armament of nine 12-inch (30.5cm) guns and thinner armor than battleships for less weight and more speed. Intended to destroy Japanese cruisers, they spent the war enhancing the carriers' antiaircraft defenses.

Left: Captain Theodore C. Aylward, acting commander of Task Force 52's Gunboat Support Group, observes amphibious maneuvers in the Hawaiian Islands from the bridge of his landing ship, infantry, fleet flagship, LCFF-988, late in 1944. First seeing active service as the commanding officer of the submarine Searaven (SS-196) in the early months of the war, Aylward led his support group during the invasions of both Iwo Jima and Okinawa.

Above: Some of 12 LCVPs (landing craft, vehicle, personnel) that had been brought in by the attack transport *Sanborn* (APA-193) make their way toward Iwo Jima on February 18, 1945. Iwo, with an airfield that could accommodate damaged B-29s unable to return to the Marianas and that would serve as a base for fighter escorts, was of strategic importance, but its 22,785 defenders, brilliantly commanded by Lieutenant General Tadamichi Kuribayashi, had prepared an extensive network of defenses throughout the island.

Left: The first wave of marines comes ashore and is quickly pinned down on February 18, 1945, in footage that appeared in the documentary film, *From the Shores of Iwo Jima.* In accordance with his plan to inflict maximum casualties on the Americans, General Kuribayashi waited for the first waves to come ashore and congregate before unleashing the heavy ordnance that had lay hidden within the tunnels of Mount Suribachi.

"If America's casualties are high enough, Washington will think twice before launching another invasion against Japanese territory."

—*Lieutenant General Tadamichi Kuribayashi, declaring his goal for defending Iwo Jima.*

Left: Amphibious tractors and other landing craft pass Mount Suribachi as they bring reinforcements to the beachhead on Iwo on February 19, 1945. Although the "amtracs" could drive right up onto the beach, they soon found the fine volcanic sand difficult going, even for tracked vehicles. Those that stalled, or were wrecked by Japanese guns, interfered with others trying to clear the beachhead.

Right: A US tanker goes up in smoke and flame as a result of enemy action off Iwo Jima. In addition to the marine casualties, the navy lying offshore suffered destruction on February 21, when six suicide planes badly damaged the carrier *Saratoga*, which lost 123 men killed or missing, and two others sank the escort carrier *Bismarck Sea*, with 318 of its crew.

Below: A broached LCM (landing craft, mechanized) from attack transport *Belle Grove* is in center foreground. Several LVTs (landing vehicles, tracked) also litter the beach amid scattered supplies and mounds of volcanic ash, while marines fight their way to the airfield and toward Suribachi. The marines called Iwo hell, to which navy photographer Paul Guttman, recalling the sulfurous fumes that emanated from it, added, "It even smelled like hell."

Above: Five marines and a navy corpsman raise a second flag above Mount Suribachi on February 24, 1945. The first flag was judged too small to be seen by the ships and planes supporting the marines, with the possible consequence of their bombarding the men who had just reached the 545-foot (152.5m) summit. For that reason—not primarily for propaganda value—a larger flag was brought up.

Above: The second flag is secured atop Mount Suribachi. Joe Rosenthal's picture of the second flag raising quickly became a Marine Corps icon, but fighting continued unabated across the rest of the island until March 26, when organized resistance ended; Kuribayashi committed suicide and his body was hidden. Only 219 of Iwo's defenders surrendered; the rest died after having killed 6,821 Americans and wounded another 19,217.

Right: Among the many aircraft operating from Iwo Jima's airfield were this Northrop P-61B Black Widow of the 548th Night Fighter Squadron (left) and a Lockheed F-5, the photoreconnaissance version of the P-38L Lightning. Patrolling the B-29 routes, the 548th shot down five Japanese planes, and on the night of August 14, 1945, one of its Black Widows reportedly drove a Ki.43 into the sea, contending for the last, albeit unofficial, aerial victory of the war.

Left: Battleship *South Dakota* steams through heavy seas while en route to the Fifth Fleet's second raid on Tokyo for the month, February 24, 1945. Intended to divert enemy attention and hinder any effort to support the defenders on Iwo Jima, the first such strike, on February 16, marked the first time carrier-launched aircraft had bombed the Japanese capital since the Doolittle Raid on April 18, 1942.

Opposite: Gunner's Mate First Class Carrick Thomas passes a clip of four 40mm rounds from *Alaska*'s magazine through a hatch to the antiaircraft guns above in March 1945. On March 18 the Fifth Fleet attacked air bases and other installations in southern Kyushu, followed by raids on Kobe Harbor and other targets on Honshu the next day. Most of the Japanese planes that tried to strike back were shot down by carrier fighters or antiaircraft gunfire.

Right: Marine Privates First Class H. J. Zukowski and Samuel Paladins stand watch beneath the 40mm antiaircraft guns aboard aircraft carrier *Randolph*. Entering combat with the Iwo Jima operation, *Randolph* was back at Ulithi Atoll in the Palau Islands on March 11, 1945, when a lone Yokosuka P1Y1 bomber crashed into its side, killing 25 men and wounding 106. Repaired at Ulithi, *Randolph* returned to action at Okinawa on April 7.

——*Paul Guttman, on how he overcame fear in combat.*

Left: Photographer's Mate Second Class Paul D. Guttman took this photograph of a Yokosuka P1Y1 bomber about to crash after being hit by antiaircraft fire during Task Force 58's carrier strikes on the Japanese home islands on March 19, 1945. The only Japanese success occurred when a dive bomber slipped in to score two 550-pound (249.5kg) bomb hits on the carrier *Franklin*.

Paul D. Guttman (1920–2005)

A member of the New York National Guard before the war, Paul Dennis Guttman lied his way past eye and ear deficiencies to join the US Navy's 59th Construction Battalion, but his camera work got him detached to serve on Edward Steichen's Naval Aviation Photo Unit. His and the work of fellow enlisted cameramen generally did not get the individual acknowledgment afforded officers on Steichen's team, entering the archives simply as "US Navy." Nevertheless, taking on a variety of assignments on land, air, and sea—and for several weeks under the sea aboard the submarine *Spot*—Guttman carried his camera into harm's way from Kwajalein in January 1944 through Okinawa in June 1945. Most of his still photos were black and white, his color primarily being motion pictures, some of which, taken aboard the carrier *Yorktown*, were used in the wartime film, *Men of the Fighting Lady*. In the course of that work, he shared credit in shooting down three enemy aircraft and was awarded the Silver Star, Distinguished Flying Cross, and the Submarine Combat Badge.

Left: Photographer's Mate Second Class Paul Guttman takes five beside a medical tent somewhere in the Pacific, with his motion picture camera, camera bag, and steel helmet close at hand. (Paul D. Guttman)

Right: *Franklin* moves up the East River toward the New York Navy Yard on April 28, 1945, after returning from its ordeal off Japan. One of the bombs that hit the ship penetrated two decks aft, but the other penetrated the flight deck centerline among aircraft that had been fueled and armed, causing fires that almost sank *Franklin* and killed 724 men and injured 265.

Below: A forward view as *Franklin* approaches Manhattan shows the damage to the flight deck. The 704 crewmen who did not abandon ship succeeded in getting *Franklin's* fires under control. Two, Chaplain Lieutenant Commander Joseph T. Callahan and Lieutenant Junior Grade Donald A. Gary, were awarded the Medal of Honor for their actions. Although repaired and recommissioned, *Franklin* never went to sea again.

Above: Destroyer *Halsey Powell* (DD-686) comes alongside the *Iowa*-class battleship *Wisconsin* (BB-64) to refuel on February 27, 1945. During the February 16 raid on Japan, *Halsey Powell* shot down a Japanese plane. On March 20, an enemy plane missed carrier *Hancock* but struck the nearby *Halsey Powell*, jamming its steering gear, killing nine crewmen and wounding 30. Quick action by the crew prevented a collision, and *Halsey Powell* reached Ulithi for repairs on March 25.

Opposite top: Eastern Aircraft-built TBM-1 Avengers and Curtiss SB2C-4 Helldivers of Air Group 2 line the afterdeck of carrier *Hornet* (CV-12) in March 1945, as a new fleet carrier, *Bonnehomme Richard* (CV-31), arrives to participate in Operation Iceberg, the invasion of Okinawa. Two light carriers can be seen in the background. *Bonnehome Richard* would serve throughout the campaign and in Operation Magic Carpet, the return of service personnel home after the war.

Opposite bottom: Antiaircraft gunners practice at their 40mm AA gun mounts aboard the escort carrier *Makin Island* (CVE-93) on March 21, shortly before steaming to its station off the invasion beach at Okinawa. A veteran of Leyte, Lingayen Gulf—where a sister ship, *Ommaney Bay* (CVE-79), was sunk after taking a kamikaze hit from a Yokosuka P1Y1 on January 4, 1945—and Iwo Jima, *Makin Island* supported the Okinawa operation, with its aircraft carrying out more than 2,250 combat sorties.

The Mariners of Kerama

On March 26, 1945, troops of the 77th Infantry Division made the first of 15 landings in the Kerama Retto, 15 miles (24km) west of Okinawa, and completed their seizure of the island group on the twenty-ninth. Besides serving as an anchorage for the Okinawa campaign, Kerama hosted Patrol Bombing Squadrons VPB-18, -21, -26, -27 and -208, and Air Sea Rescue Squadron VH-3, all equipped with Martin PBM Mariner flying boats, VPB-13, which used Consolidated PB2Y-5 Coronados, and their attendant seaplane tenders, *Bering Strait, Chandeleur, Hamlin, Onslow, Saint George, Shelikof,* and *Yakutat*.

Although it never replaced the PBY Catalina, the PBM Mariner was a better performer, with a speed of 205 mph (330kph) and a range of 3,000 miles (4,800km). Besides 4,000 pounds (1,815kg) of bombs or two torpedoes, the Mariner's three twin turrets and two fuselage hatch positions mounted a total of eight .50-caliber machine guns. Throughout the Okinawa campaign the PBMs patrolled for submarines, attacked enemy shipping, and rescued scores of downed airmen.

Above: A PBM of VPB-27 refuels from a fuel bowser boat in Tanapag Harbor, Saipan, in May 1945 before starting out on the 14-hour flight to the squadron's combat base at Kerama.

Above right: Members of VPB-27 sit atop their PBM's wing at Tanapag in April 1945. VPB-27's only loss occurred while attacking Japanese shipping off Formosa on August 7, when two planes were shot down, with all 24 crewmen killed.

Opposite: A PBM-5 of VPB-27 undergoes engine maintenance at Tanapag. On March 23 the squadron was ordered to Kerama Retto, where it would be serviced by seaplane tenders *Onslow*, *Shelikof,* and *Yakutat*.

Right: A VPB-27 Mariner is lifted by the stern crane of a large seaplane tender at Kerama. *Pine Island* and the auxiliary seaplane tender *Saint George* were capable of taking the flying boats aboard for extensive work if necessary.

Left: Battleship *Idaho* fires its 14-inch (35.5cm) guns at almost point-blank range to clear the beach at Okinawa on April 1, 1945. The warship, which had supported a multitude of Pacific landings since Attu in May 1943, also provided AA defense off Okinawa, downing five suicide planes on April 12 before a near miss damaged its port blisters. After repairs at Guam, *Idaho* returned to Okinawa on May 22 and continued support until June 20.

Above: The Fifth Fleet lies offshore while the Americans consolidate the beachhead at Okinawa. Telephone lines can be seen strung from the trees. Lieutenant General Mitsuru Ushijima eschewed a beach defense in favor of drawing the US Army and Marine troops inland, to be worn down as his 120,000-man Thirty-Second Army conducted a fighting retreat into the southern portion of the island.

"I was scared as hell but also proud to be with those going into combat . . . I was going to do this thing, and if I got through it, which I doubted, maybe life would be different when I got home."

—*Private Thomas Hannaher, US Marine Corps, recalling his thoughts during the Okinawa landing, April 1, 1945.*

Left: Japanese airmen reenact, postwar, the ceremony that preceded a *kamikaze* ("divine wind") mission. Starting in 1944, Japanese suicide attacks by air, land, and sea reached a crescendo at Okinawa, including waves of aircraft called *kikusui* ("floating chrysanthemums"), explosive-packed one-man *Shinyo* ("ocean shaker") boats, and an airplane belly landing on Yontan airfield, on the night of May 24–25, that disgorged grenade-armed *Giretsu* ("heroic") commandos who destroyed seven planes and two 70,000-gallon fuel tanks before being killed off.

Below: Machinist's Mate Third Class K. A. Meredith tapes two pinups to the bulkhead of his TBM Avenger in anticipation of a long mission from carrier *Bennington* (CV-20). Joining Task Group 58.1 on February 8, 1945, *Bennington* supported both the Iwo Jima and Okinawa operations. When a PBM-5 Mariner of VPB-21 spotted the mammoth battleship *Yamato* and its escorts in the East China Sea on April 7, *Bennington*'s were among more than 1,000 planes from a total of 10 carriers that attacked the Japanese force.

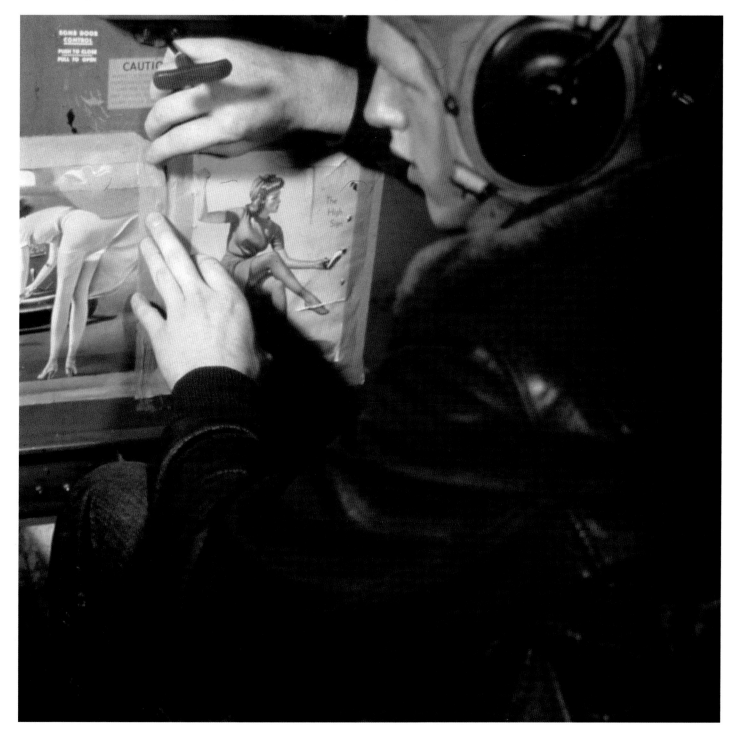

Left: An officer aboard *Bennington* dedicates a bomb to a slain shipmate before delivering it to the Japanese. Marine F4U-1D pilot Lieutenant Kenneth E. Huntington of *Bennington*-based VMF-112 and an SB2C of VB-82 scored the first two hits on *Yamato*, destroying its radar and starting a fire. After five bomb and ten torpedo hits, the world's largest battleship sank, along with light cruiser *Yahagi* and four destroyers. Ten American planes were lost, including a VB-82 Helldiver.

Opposite top: Marines load a one-man *Shinyo* ("ocean shaker") boat aboard an amphibious tractor on Okinawa. Some 700 explosives-laden *Shinyo* boats were committed to the Okinawa campaign, but all that their suicide missions achieved were to sink two vessels—landing ship, mechanized, LSM-12, which was hit on March 31 and foundered on April 4, and landing craft, infantry, gunboat, LCI(G)-82, sunk on April 4—and damage five vessels.

Opposite: LCS(L)-3-33 leads a column of other landing craft, support (large), Mark IIIs, toward Okinawa. A veteran of Iwo Jima, LCS(L)-3-33 was on Rader Picket Station Number 1 on April 12, 1945, when three Aichi D3A2s made a suicide attack on it. It shot down the first, the second sheered off its radio antenna before crashing into the sea, but the third kamikaze struck home, and the crew abandoned ship before LCS(L)-3-33 exploded.

"She was covered with clouds of black smoke. We flew low over the area and saw hundreds clinging to the wreckage. They never had a chance. It looked like there were no rafts or lifeboats. And that ship—I knew she was the enemy and we'd hunted her for years—but God, she was a beautiful thing. No one who saw her will ever forget her."

—Lieutenant Junior Grade Richard L. Simms of US Navy Patrol Squadron VPB-21, whose Martin PBM-5 Mariner crew first spotted battleship Yamato and watched as carrier planes sank it on April 7, 1945.

Franklin D. Roosevelt (1882–1945)

Taking office amid the Great Depression in 1933, Franklin Delano Roosevelt had seen the United States through the financial crisis, and the world war that followed it, with a combination of optimism and activism. The only president to serve more than two terms, "FDR" was the only national leader that a young generation of servicemen had known as they looked forward to the last year of the conflict. On April 12, 1945, Roosevelt was sitting for a portrait by artist Elizabeth Shoumatoff, who told him the painting would be completed in about a quarter of an hour when he complained of a sharp pain in the back of his head, then slumped forward in his chair. Moments later the thirty-second president of the United States was dead from a cerebral hemorrhage. His passing came at the start of the largest and bloodiest island battle of the Pacific War, and left his successor, Harry S. Truman, with a major role to play, for which he seemed little prepared.

Below: Standing before a flag at half-mast, marines at Naval Air Station Alameda attend memorial services for Roosevelt on April 15, 1945. All over the United States and among the armed forces overseas, his death was received with shock and almost universal mourning. In Berlin, Adolf Hitler celebrated the news as a turning point in the war—until a thunderclap of Soviet artillery showed him it was not.

Above: Sworn in as vice president on January 20, 1945, Harry S. Truman held that post only 82 days, during which President Franklin D. Roosevelt had rarely informed him of any decisions, let alone consulting him on them. Upon taking office as president, he retained Roosevelt's entire cabinet, with the understanding that he would make the ultimate decisions with expectations of the cabinet's full support on those decisions.

"Boys, if you ever pray, pray for me now. I don't know if you fellas ever had a load of hay fall on you, but when they told me what happened yesterday, I felt like the moon and the stars and all the planets had fallen on me."

—Harry S. Truman to news reporters, April 13, 1945.

"At this spot the 77th Infantry Division lost a buddy, Ernie Pyle, April 18, 1944."

—*Monument on Ie Shima where Pulitzer Prize-winning war correspondent Ernie Pyle was killed by Japanese gunfire.*

Opposite: Marine sentries guard the flag, still flying at half-mast in Roosevelt's honor as it would for a full month after his death, on the northern tip of Okinawa on May 6, 1945. In contrast to Hitler's glee upon learning of Roosevelt's death, Japanese Prime Minister Kantaro Suzuki publicly expressed his condolences, and Radio Tokyo called Roosevelt "a great man— one of the greatest statesmen."

Right: Steaming off Ie Shima on April 16, the destroyer *Isherwood* engaged a Nakajima Ki.43 fighter, which fell into the sea aft of the battleship *Texas*. Subsequently dispatched to the radar picket line north of Okinawa, *Isherwood* was crashed on April 22 by an Aichi D3A1, which caused fires and a secondary explosion in a depth charge rack that killed or injured 80 crewmen.

Kikusui Crash Bill

The massed *Kikusui* or "floating chrysanthemum" attacks on the Allied fleets around Okinawa involved as many as 350 aircraft at a time, either being deliberately dived into ships by their pilots or escorting the kamikazes.

Although they failed to sink a single fleet carrier, battleship, or cruiser, the 1,465 known suicide planes took a heavy toll on the smaller warships, sinking at least 30 along with three victory ships, damaging another 368 vessels, killing 4,900 seamen and wounding another 4,600. Although the kamikazes were instructed to try to reach the carriers and plunge into their elevators for maximum effect, that proved easier said than done—when facing intense AA fire and swarms of American fighters, most suicide pilots went after the first warships they found, which most of the time were the destroyers on the fleet's radar picket line. Consequently, 14 destroyers fell victim to kamikazes, and numerous others survived harrowing ordeals with heavy damage and grim casualties.

Below: On May 5, crewmen clear debris and repair damage aboard the escort carrier *Sangamon* (CVE-26) after a kamikaze dropped its bomb and crashed into the deck off Kerama Retto the night before, resulting in fires, 11 crewmen dead, 25 missing, and 21 seriously injured.

Above: Marine First Lieutenant Jeremiah O'Keefe of VMF-323 indicates five enemy planes downed in his first combat, on April 22, 1945. Flying F4U-1Ds from Kadena Field, Okinawa, VMF-323 claimed 124.5 victories and produced seven aces without losing a man.

Above left: Lookouts watch for enemy planes off Ie Shima on April 16, 1945. In the Okinawa campaign's third *kikusui* attack on April 15–16, destroyer *Pringle* (DD-477) was sunk, and six ships damaged. *Laffey* (DD-724) survived five kamikaze and three bomb hits, and is preserved at the Patriots Point Naval and Maritime Museum in South Carolina.

Left: *Bunker Hill,* Vice Admiral Marc Mitscher's Task Force 58 flagship, after an A6M5 Zero and a Yokosuka D4Y3 dive bomber bombed and crashed into it on May 11. *Bunker Hill* burned for 24 hours, 396 crewmen were killed or missing, and 288 were wounded.

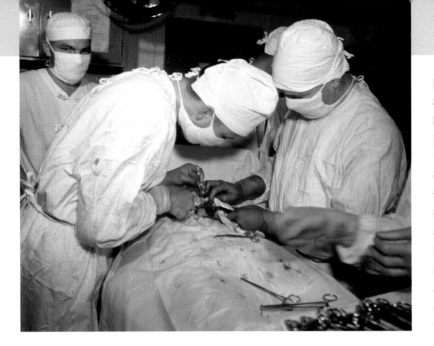

Right: Lieutenant Junior Grade Williams performs an epigastric hernia operation on Electrician's Mate First Class Carey Couron aboard carrier *Randolph* in May 1945. Assisting are Lieutenant Commander James, anesthetist Lieutenant Robertson, and Pharmacist's Mate Second Class George Fritch. Even while the battle casualties came in, shipboard medical facilities had to be prepared for any exigencies to keep their crews at maximum efficiency.

Below: A flamethrowing M4A3R3 Sherman tank hurls a jet of blazing oil during maneuvers at Fort Benning, Georgia, in May 1945. Developed by the Army Chemical Warfare Service, the flamethrower device fit into the hull machine gun mount in front of the turret. Dubbed the "Zippo" by the Americans, the M4A3R3 saw extensive use against dug-in Japanese positions on Iwo Jima and Okinawa, averting the need to storm them.

"When a kamikaze hits a US carrier it means six months of repair at Pearl. When a kamikaze hits a Limey carrier it's just a case of 'Sweepers, man your brooms.'"

—A US Navy liaison officer aboard HMS Indefatigable, May 1945.

Left: Admiral Sir Bruce Fraser commanded Britain's Eastern Fleet and Task Force 57, which was attached to the US Fifth Fleet during the Okinawa campaign, primarily engaged in eliminating air bases in Sakashima Gunto to the southwest. Kamikazes staging from those islands hit some of the British carriers, but thanks to their armored flight decks only Victorious suffered significant damage. Fraser signed the Japanese surrender documents on Britain's behalf on September 2, 1945.

Below: Battleship Howe, flagship of Admiral Sir Bruce Fraser, passes through the Suez Canal en route to join the Eastern Fleet. Between March 26 and May 25, 1945, Howe and King George V supported carriers in operations against Sakashima Gunto. On May 4 the battleships bombarded Hiara and Miyako Jima, during which a kamikaze glanced off Howe's armored hull, crashed in the sea and exploded.

Opposite: A navy corpsman attends to an injured marine on Okinawa. Some of the fiercest fighting was along the Shuri Line, which included the current capital of Naha, the ancient capital of Shuri, and hotly contested strongpoints such as Sugar Loaf Hill. On May 29 the 22nd Marine Regiment secured Naha, and an element of the 5th Marines took Shuri Castle. With the line breached, surviving Japanese withdrew south.

Top right: Military ambulances line up near the docks at Guam, awaiting the arrival of the hospital ship *Solace* with casualties from Okinawa on June 4, 1945. At that time General Ushijima's Thirty-Second Army had withdrawn from the Shuri Line, reduced from 50,000 troops at the start of the operation to 30,000. On June 11, the Japanese were driven to the Kiyan Peninsula on the southern tip of the island, where they made their final stand.

Right: Admiral Chester W. Nimitz and Admiral Raymond A. Spruance walk with army, navy, and marine officers on Okinawa in the spring of 1945. On May 27, Admiral William Halsey relieved Spruance of command, and the Fifth became the Third Fleet again. On June 5, Halsey's fleet ran afoul of another typhoon, which tore the bow off the heavy cruiser *Pittsburgh*, and buckled the forward flight decks of carriers *Hornet* and *Bennington*.

"Among other damage, *Hornet*'s flight deck got folded down around the bow. After that the ship reversed course and we launched over the stern."

—John Theodore Crosby, F6F-5 pilot, VF-17, recalling how carrier Hornet was affected by the typhoon of June 5, 1945.

Right: A flight deck handler on carrier *Bennington*, wearing life jacket and helmet, makes an adjustment to his equipment in 1945. Arriving at Leyte on June 12 to have the typhoon damage to its forward flight deck repaired, *Bennington* departed on July 1, and rejoined the Third Fleet on July 10 to participate in air strikes on air bases and seaports throughout the Japanese home islands.

"Our strategy, tactics, and techniques were all used to the utmost. We fought valiantly, but it was as nothing before the material strength of the enemy."

—*Final message from Major General Isamu Cho, chief of staff, Japanese Thirty-Second Army on Okinawa, before committing seppuku on June 22, 1945.*

Right: A GI finds a moment to shave as the battle for Okinawa nears its conclusion. On June 18 the Tenth Army commander, Lieutenant General Simon Bolivar Buckner Jr., was visiting advancing marines when a Japanese 47mm-shell hit drove a coral fragment into his heart. He was the highest-ranking American officer to die in combat. As organized resistance broke down, Ushijima and his chief of staff, Major General Isamu Cho, committed ritual suicide on June 22.

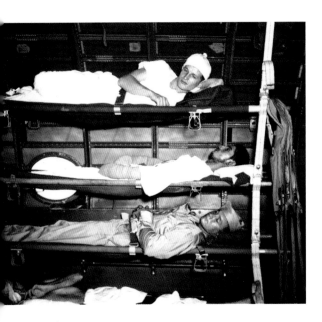

Above: Willey Edwards, Joseph Gonzales, and George Stillwell await evacuation by plane from Okinawa to Guam for medical attention. The Okinawa campaign cost the US Army and Marines 7,613 killed or missing and 34,116 wounded, while the navy lost 36 ships sunk and 368 damaged, with 4,900 sailors dead or missing and 4,800 wounded. A total of 763 aircraft were lost. British Task Force 57 suffered four ships damaged, 98 planes lost, 62 dead and 82 wounded.

Opposite: Members of an M5A1 light tank crew (right) try to assist crewmen trapped inside an M4 medium tank, on its back and burning after hitting a land mine during the continuing fighting on Okinawa in June 1945. Lacking comparable armor, the Japanese fought the M4 Shermans with 47mm antitank guns, artillery, and suicide squads armed with Model 97 grenades, 22-pound (10kg) satchel charges, and Model 99 magnetic demolition charges.

April 30, 1945 *Adolf Hitler commits suicide. After a vain attempt to negotiate with Soviet forces on May 1, propaganda minister Josef Goebbels has his children poisoned, then he and his wife commit suicide.*

May 2, 1945 *General Helmuth Weidling, commander of the LVI Panzer Corps, surrenders Berlin to General Vassily Chuikov, commander of the Soviet Eighth Guards Army.*

May 4, 1945 *German forces in northwest Germany, Denmark, and the Netherlands surrender to Field Marshal Sir Bernard Law Montgomery at Lüneburg Heath.*

May 7–9, 1945 *Germany signs a general unconditional surrender with General Dwight D. Eisenhower at Reims on May 7, and with Soviet forces in Berlin on May 9.*

Left: Chinese-manned M3A3 light tanks cross a bridge en route to their objective. In March 1945, the Japanese launched an offensive aiming for the Fourteenth Air Force's air base at Chihchiang and possibly Chiang Kai-shek's capital of Chunking. This time, however, their opposition included 36 American-advised, trained and supplied Chinese divisions, collectively called Alpha Force, which stopped the Japanese near Wu-yang on May 5–6, and then began a counteroffensive that the Chinese would sustain to the end of the war.

Above: US Army infantrymen conduct an Okinawan woman to the rear. Japanese dead on Okinawa are estimated at 66,000, with 7,400 combatants captured along with 3,400 unarmed laborers. Of the 7,830 Japanese aircraft destroyed, 4,155 were in combat, 2,655 operationally and 1,020 on the ground. More than 4,600 aircrewmen died in suicide missions, and about 3,650 sailors perished in the *Yamato* sortie. Postwar studies estimated the civilian death toll at more than 122,000.

Above: Troops of Company E, 129th Regiment, 37th Division ride tanks across the Cagayan River as they move up to seize Tuguegarao City and its airfield on June 25, 1945. The regiment secured Aparri between June 26 and 27. Organized resistance in the Cagayan Valley ceased at the end of the month, but the Americans continued mopping up pockets of Japanese into August, while General Tomoyuki Yamashita withdrew his 52,000 remaining troops into the Sierra Madre.

Left: A 155mm self-propelled howitzer and ammunition train of the 135th Field Artillery, part of Major General Robert S. Beighton's 37th Infantry Division, advances northward up Route 5 toward Ilagan in Luzon's Cagayan Valley. The Cagayan campaign began on May 31, and on June 14 the 37th Division killed 437 Japanese for the loss of two soldiers, securing Cagayan on the sixteenth. Ilagan fell soon after, and the 37th fought off a counterattack at San Antonio on the nineteenth.

Opposite: A Republic P-47D-30-RE Thunderbolt of *Escuadrón Aérea de Pelea* 201 flies over Manila. After U-boats sank four of its tankers, Mexico declared war on Germany on May 22, 1942, but its principal contribution to the Allied war effort was *Escuadrón* 201, consisting of 25 P-47s, 30 pilots, and 300 ground personnel, attached to the 58th Fighter Group, Fifth Air Force in the Philippines.

Left: A P-47D-23-RE of the 311th Squadron, 58th Fighter Group returns from bombing a target at Santiago, northern Luzon. The black-and-white recognition bands and red, white, and blue tail stripes were applied to Far East Air Forces fighters operating in the Philippine Archipelago in January 1945. With most aerial opposition in the islands themselves completely eliminated, the fighters were primarily engaged in ground support.

Below: Captain Jesus Blanco, intelligence officer of *Escuadrón* 201, briefs pilots for a sortie from Porac Strip on Clark Field, Luzon, in July 1945.

Calling themselves the "Aztec Eagles," *Escuadrón* 201's pilots flew about 90 combat missions, including 53 in support of the 25th Infantry

Division, during its breakout through the Cagayan Valley from June 4 to July 4, 1945, and five fighter sweeps over Formosa on July 6–9 and August 8.

Above: Projectiles launched from navy landing craft, infantry (rocket), LCI(R)-338, streak toward Labuan Island in Brunei Bay prior to the Australian 9th Division's landing on June 10, 1945. The Allied liberation of Borneo began on May 1 with the landing of the Australian 26th Brigade on Tarakan Island, whose last defenses fell on June 21, at a cost of more than 200 Australian dead. Labuan cost more than 100 Australian lives.

Left: General Douglas MacArthur, Lieutenant General Leslie Morshead, I Australian Corps, Air Vice Marshal W. D. Bostock, Royal Australian Air Force, and Vice Admiral Daniel E. Barbey, US Navy Amphibious Forces, visit the Balikpapan beachhead. On July 1, 33,000 troops of the Australian 7th Division, with American and Dutch troops and naval support, landed north of Balikpapan in the largest amphibious operation in Australian history. Good preparation kept casualties low, and the last organized resistance ended on the twenty-first.

Chapter 6

Setting Sun

The fall of Imperial Japan

Opposite: One of thousands of American servicemen redeploying from Europe to the Pacific for the invasion of Japan in the spring of 1945, Combat Engineer Private First Class Royland Otter takes a last look at France before boarding ship near Marseille. "As long as it had to happen," Otter remarked, "it would have been nicer to have gone through the States to see my wife and three daughters, but it's too late now."

By the end of June 1945, Japan was the last Axis power in play, and standing very much alone amid a crumbling empire. The Americans had secured Okinawa and most of Luzon. The British had retaken Rangoon and were moving on Singapore. Even in China the Japanese army's last offensive had been stopped on May 5, and by June 7 it was back at its starting point, with the Chinese still advancing.

Overriding all of those setbacks was the grim reality of total war being brought to the Japanese homeland. American submarines had virtually choked off the influx of vitally needed resources by sea. B-29s from the Marianas regularly bombed Japanese cities, inflicting devastating losses in lives and property. Iwo Jima and the newly captured airfields on Okinawa provided damaged B-29s with an interim safe haven as well as bases from which fighters could escort the bombers. On top of that, carrier planes intermittently raided port facilities, sinking what remained of the Imperial Navy in their harbors.

Still, die-hard Japanese militarists looked forward to the final battle, training the populace to resist an Allied invasion to the death in a reprise of Iwo Jima and Okinawa on the national scale, while clinging to the possibility that the already apparent differences between the West and the Soviet Union might yet turn the tide in their favor. Two events ultimately dashed even those forlorn hopes. On August 6 and 9, the Americans unleashed the power of two atomic bombs on the cities of Hiroshima and Nagasaki. On August 8 the Soviet Union, as it promised the Western Allies it would do three months after Germany's capitulation, declared war on Japan and swiftly overwhelmed its armies in Manchuria and Korea.

On August 14, Emperor Hirohito agreed to unconditional surrender, which was formally signed aboard USS *Missouri* on September 2, 1945, World War II was over.

Above: Boeing B-29s on a Marianas air base sit with their bomb bays open, waiting for ground crews to load them up with high explosive or incendiary ordnance for the next mission to major industrial centers in Japan. The capture of Saipan, Guam, and Tinian, and the expansion of their airfields by the Seabees, made it possible to transfer the XX Bomber Command over from China to join the XXI Bomber Command in a single, concentrated Twentieth Air Force.

Curtis E. LeMay (1906–1990)

Curtis Emerson LeMay spent his childhood traveling and working around the country before he graduated from Ohio State University and joined the US Army Air Corps Reserve in October 1929. He was initially a pursuit pilot, but LeMay's navigational talents led him to fly bombers through most of the 1930s and in World War II with the Eighth Air Force, with which he rose to colonel leading the 3rd Bomb Division. In August 1944, LeMay was transferred to China to lead the B-29-equipped XX Bomber Command, later moving to XXI Bomber Command in the Marianas in January 1945, and ultimately taking command of the Twentieth Air Force as a major general. After the war LeMay led the Strategic Air Command, became the youngest American general to receive his fourth star—in 1951, at age 44—and rose to chief of staff of the US Air Force before retiring in February 1965, subsequently making a failed vice presidential bid with George Wallace's American Independent Party in 1968.

Left: Nose art became an almost ubiquitous feature on American warplanes, especially bombers. The Consolidated B-24, with its flat sides, made an ideal canvas on which talented ground crewmen could paint their fancies or fantasies, but the cockpit area of the B-29, while rounder, was even larger. The crew of B-29 42-63512 *Nip Clipper* of the 9th Bomb Group had to bail out on May 22, 1945, after its number two engine was shot out and then the number four engine quit.

"Flying fighters is fun.
Flying bombers is important."

—*Major General Curtis E. LeMay.*

October 18, 1945 *The International Military Tribunal begins the trial of 24 Nazi war criminals in the Palace of Justice at Nuremberg. This results in five acquittals and 19 convictions, including 12 with the death penalty.*

October 24, 1945 *United Nations Organization, conceived in 1942 to replace the League of Nations, is officially founded, with permanent members the United States, United Kingdom, Soviet Union, Republic of China, and France, as well as 46 other sovereign nations.*

January 17, 1946 *United Nations, officially founded on October 24, 1945, with an initial complement of 46 countries, conducts its first meeting in Westminster Central Hall, London.*

October 16, 1946 *Ten of 12 convicted Nazi war criminals are hanged at Nuremberg. The exceptions are Hermann Göring, who committed suicide the night before, and Martin Bormann, whose remains in Berlin were identified in 1972.*

Opposite: Marine Private First Class Ransdall W. "Bud" Sprenger—dubbed the "Marianas Michelangelo" for his skill at transferring female pinups from the pages of *Esquire* magazine to the sides of more than a dozen Superfortresses—touches up B-29 42-24596 of the 869th Squadron, 497th Bomb Group on Saipan in February 1945. *Little Gem* survived the war and remained in service until reclaimed at Tinker Air Force Base on May 10, 1949.

Right: Another innovation that made the B-29 a "Superfortress" was its remotely controlled .50-caliber machine gun turrets such as this one, whose gunner peers from the domed side window in the aft fuselage as he operates the gunsight. The author's father, Paul Guttman, flew three missions in B-29s occupying this position, alternating between photographing the mission and engaging enemy fighters.

Right: The bombardier looks back from the nose of a B-29 en route to Japan. The most complex piece of technology to see service with the US Army Air Forces, the B-29 featured a pressurized, heated fuselage interior that allowed crewmen to perform their duties unencumbered by cold-weather clothing or oxygen masks. They needed that comfort, because they were flying considerably longer sorties than the average B-17 or B-24 crew.

Right: The radio operator on a B-29 confirms a message while a crewman looks in. His equipment included a shortwave "liaison" receiver for contact with ground bases thousands of miles away, "command" equipment for communicating with accompanying aircraft, a high-frequency (HF) transmitter, a very high-frequency (VHF) transceiver, and Morse code equipment for situations in which voice communication was undesirable or impossible.

Above: The gunner and an aerial photographer peer out of the left waist gunner's position on a B-24 of the 308th Bomb Group at the start of a mission. After flying its last offensive sorties with the Fourteenth Air Force in China, early in June 1945 the 308th Group withdrew to bases in Rupsi and Tezpur, India, from which its Liberators would be engaged primarily in flying supplies to China over the Hump. The group returned to the United States in December.

Right: A Japanese city displays the effectiveness of the tactics adopted by Curtis LeMay after taking over XXI Bomber Command on January 20, 1945. Judging high-altitude formation bombing in the face of jet stream winds and cloud cover ineffective, LeMay ordered low-level incendiary attacks by bomber streams at night against the predominantly wood-and-paper dwellings in Japanese cities. The deadliest strike, against Tokyo on March 10, killed 100,000 civilians and destroyed 250,000 buildings.

Below: B-29s of the 5th Squadron, 9th Group, 313th Bomb Wing, operating from North Field, Tinian, embark on a mission in July 1945. By then, LeMay had assigned the 313th Wing, with its four groups and 160 planes, to carry out Operation Starvation, dropping mines off the coast and in the waterways of the home islands to hinder whatever maritime traffic got past American submarines.

Right: A sailor polishes the fuselage of a newly delivered Consolidated PB2Y-2 Privateer patrol bomber at a Philippine base in 1945. Developed from the navy version of the B-24 Liberator, the PB4Y-1, the PB4Y-2 featured a lengthened fuselage with a single large vertical stabilizer and rudder. It also dispensed with turbosuper-charged engines, since it was not intended for high altitude, and had a formidable defensive armament of 12 .50-caliber machine guns, as well as up to 12,800 pounds (5,800kg) of explosive ordnance.

"The 'Frank' is a very maneuverable ship, but we could outrun it and outdive it. No one tried to outclimb it."

—*Major Edward S. Popek, 342nd Squadron, 348th Fighter Group, who downed a Ki.84 after a difficult combat on August 1, 1945, for his fifth and last victory.*

Below: A Nakajima Ki.84 *Hayate* ("Gale"), the Japanese army's best fighter (code-named "Frank" by the Allies) of the 1st *Chutai* (squadron), 85th *Sentai*, sits before another Ki.84 of the 22nd *Sentai* and a row of earlier Ki.43 *Hayabusa* ("Peregrine Falcon") fighters (Allied codename "Oscar") at Kimpo Air Base, Korea. First to use the *Hayate* in combat in China, the 22nd and 85th *Sentais* took part in one of the war's last aerial combats on August 13, 1945.

Above: P-51K-10NA 44-12017 *Mrs. Bonnie,* flown by Lieutenant Colonel William D. Dunham, deputy commander of the 348th Fighter Group, sits on Ie Shima in August 1945. By that time Mustang-equipped elements of the Fifth Air Force had moved north to support the raids on Japan. On August 1, "Dinghy" Dunham downed a Nakajima Ki.84 while escorting B-24 Liberators over Kyushu for his sixteenth and final victory.

Right: *South Dakota* crewmen watch as smoke rises from the Japan Iron and Steel Company as Task Unit 38.4.1, consisting of that battleship with *Massachusetts, Indiana,* cruisers *Chicago* and *Quincy,* and four destroyers, bombards Kamaishi on July 14, 1945. The first American shelling of Japan's home islands since 1864 began when *South Dakota* raised the signal flags "Never Forget Pearl Harbor." Among the fatalities, however, were 42 Allied prisoners engaged in forced labor at the factory.

Above: Carrier *Amagi* lies capsized and aground in 1946. Completed in August 1944, the ship saw no action before March 19, 1945, when it was damaged by American carrier planes and it was moored permanently in Kuro thereafter. Planes of Task Force 38 bombed *Amagi* again on July 24 and 28, and on the twenty-ninth the listing carrier was run aground before it capsized. The wreck was scrapped in 1947.

Left: Rear Admiral Thomas L. Sprague, commander of Task Group 38.1, receives reports from carrier *Bennington*'s officers on their latest series of strikes against Japanese shipping—which apparently went very well. Thomas Sprague had previously served with the Seventh Fleet, most notably in charge of Task Unit 77.4.1 during the critical Battle of Samar on October 25, 1944. On July 1, 1945, he left Leyte at the head of Task Group 38.1.

Battleship *Missouri*

The last American battleship to be completed was also the one on whose decks World War II would end. Laid down in the Brooklyn Navy Yard on January 6, 1941, the *Iowa*-class fast battleship *Missouri* was launched on January 29, 1944, and commissioned on June 11.

Its first operation was the Fifth Fleet's raids on Japan on February 16, after which it supported operations on Iwo Jima and Okinawa. On April 11, 1945, a Mitsubishi A6M5 Zero struck *Missouri*'s starboard side, just below main deck level, starting an oil fire and leaving a dent that remains to this day. On April 17, *Missouri* detected a submarine 12 miles (19km) off, setting off a hunt by light carrier *Bataan* and four destroyers that led to the sinking of *I-56*. On May 18, Admiral William Halsey, resuming command of the Third Fleet, boarded *Missouri* in Apra Harbor, Guam, and made it his flagship.

After the war, *Missouri* served in Korea and in Operation Desert Storm in 1991. Struck from the naval rolls in 1995, in 1998 it was memorialized at Pearl Harbor.

Opposite top: *Missouri's* Captain William M. Callaghan, Lieutenant Morris E. Eddy, and Yeoman First Class Arthur Colton stand bridge watch. When the body of the kamikaze who struck *Missouri* on April 11, 1945, was recovered, Callaghan ordered him buried at sea with military honors the next day.

Opposite bottom: Battleship *Missouri* undergoes its shakedown cruise in August 1944, with battle cruiser *Alaska* in the distance at left.

Right: *Missouri's* 5-inch (12.5cm) secondary battery performs a night firing exercise. *Missouri* had 20 such weapons in twin turrets as part of its—and the task force's—antiaircraft defense.

Above: Commander Hylan B. Lyon, *Missouri's* navigating officer, tracks the big ship's course and plots its position in the chart house during the ship's shakedown cruise.

Right: After returning from a scouting flight, with his plane hoisted by ship's crane back onto its catapult, an OS2U pilot unstraps his flight log from his leg to report to *Missouri's* intelligence officer.

Above: Survivors of the heavy cruiser *Indianapolis* (CA-35) leave the hospital ship *Tranquility* (AH-14) and are placed in ambulances on Guam on August 8, 1945. After delivering the world's first atomic bomb at Tinian on July 26, *Indianapolis* was en route to Leyte on the night of July 30, when it was hit by two torpedoes from submarine I-58 and sank in 12 minutes. Only 319 of the 1,196-man crew remained alive when finally rescued four days later. Captain Charles B. McVay III, who was among the survivors, was subsequently court-martialed.

Left: Vice Admiral Jesse B. Oldendorf rests on the bridge of his flagship, the battleship *Tennessee*, in September 1945. On August 12, Oldendorf was aboard battleship *Pennsylvania* in Buckner Bay, Okinawa, when a Japanese torpedo bomber slipped in and scored a damaging hit aft, killing 20 seamen and injuring another 10, including Oldendorf, who suffered several cracked ribs. Two days later, the task of disposing of the dead was given to *Pennsylvania's* most junior officer, the just-arrived Ensign Johnny Carson.

Left: Specialist First Class Herbert A. Rollins, the carrier pigeon handler at the Nahu Military Port in Naha, Okinawa, tends to one of his charges by the pigeon loft on August 14, 1945. Capable of relaying messages at an average speed of 60 mph (96.6kph), pigeons were still used by the US Army to convey missives, maps, and photographic film throughout World War II, with 90 percent reportedly reaching their destinations.

Above: Even while US military forces prepare nervously for Operation Olympic, the invasion of the Japanese home islands, service personnel carry on with the prosaic but vital task of sorting the mail on Okinawa. Although the events leading up to the Japanese surrender in mid-August were taken with elation and relief, the long stand-down period to follow made the moral support of letters from home no less appreciated by those still stationed overseas.

"We have discovered the most terrible bomb in the history of the world. It may be the fire destruction prophesied in the Euphrates Valley Era, after Noah and his fabulous ark."

—*President Harry S. Truman.*

Above: The B-29 *Enola Gay* of the 509th Composite Group on Tinian, flown by Colonel Paul W. Tibbets. On August 6, 1945, *Enola Gay* dropped "Little Boy," an atomic bomb, on Hiroshima. After doing so, Tibbets had been advised by J. Robert Oppenheimer, who supervised its development, to "turn either way 159 degrees. That way you get your greatest distance in the shortest length of time from the point at which the bomb explodes."

> **"The boiling pillar had become a giant mountain of jumbled rainbows. Much living substance had gone into those rainbows."**
>
> —*William L. Laurence, describing the mushroom cloud over Nagasaki in his book,* Dawn Over Zero.

Above: A view of Hiroshima, showing the destruction wrought by "Little Boy." The US Department of Energy estimated that 70,000 residents had died on the day of the bombing, but far more sobering were the aftereffects caused by the bomb's radiation, including cancer and leukemia, that were noted in subsequent observations, which raised the death toll to an estimated 200,000 by 1950.

Left: The B-29 *Bockscar* of the 393rd Squadron, 509th Composite Group was normally piloted by Captain Frederick Bock, but was flown by Major Charles W. Sweeney when it dropped a second atomic bomb, "Fat Man," on Nagasaki on August 9. Bock accompanied the mission at the controls of Captain Kermit K. Beahan's plane, *The Great Artiste*, which also carried Pulitzer Prize-winning *New York Times'* reporter William L. Laurence.

Right: October 6, 1956, Guam—A Nagasaki survivor receives treatment from an American doctor at Omura Naval Hospital on October 6, 1945. Although "Fat Man" was larger and more powerful than "Little Boy," deaths at Nagasaki were estimated at 35,000, with another 60,000 injured—much lower than at Hiroshima. Lieutenant General Jimmy Doolittle, for one, expressed satisfaction at the reduced human cost.

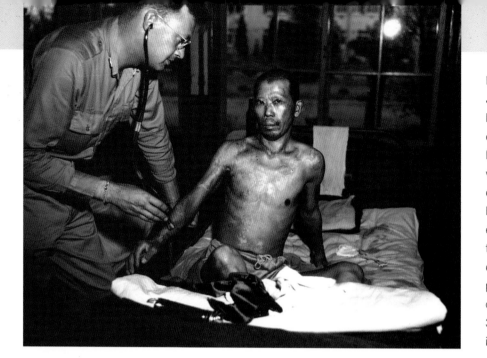

Below: In May 1946, two Japanese men salvage bricks near the ruins of a church destroyed by "Fat Man" in Nagasaki. Even with ridges and valleys dampening its effects, "Fat Man" exploded with the equivalent force of 22,000 tons (19,958 tonnes) of TNT, demolishing an estimated 44 percent of the city—an area of 2.3 by 1.9 miles (3.7 by 3.1 km), including its entire industrial district.

"I cannot bear to see my innocent people suffer any longer. Ending the war is the only way to restore world peace and to relieve the nation from the terrible distress with which it is burdened."

—*Emperor Hirohito to the Japanese Supreme Council, August 9, 1945.*

> "I knew what I was doing when I stopped the war. I have no regrets and, under the same circumstances, I would do it again."
>
> —*Harry S. Truman, looking back on his decision to drop the atomic bombs.*

Left: Clement Atlee, Harry Truman, and Josef Stalin confer at Potsdam, Germany, in July 1945 with, back row from left, American chief of staff Admiral William Leahy, British foreign minister Ernest Devin, US Secretary of State James F. Byrnes, and Soviet foreign minister Vyacheslav Molotov. As promised to the Western Allies, on August 8 the Soviet Union declared war on Japan, and the next day launched an invasion of Manchuria that swiftly destroyed Japan's Kwangtung Army, also occupying northern Korea.

Hirohito (1901–1989)

The 124th emperor of Japan was not known as Hirohito so much as by the retrospectively ironic term for the era of his reign, as Emperor Showa ("enlightened peace"). The first Japanese crown prince to travel abroad, in 1921 he visited Britain, France, Italy, the Netherlands, and Belgium.

The role of Hirohito and others of the imperial family in promulgating Japan's militarist policy and the atrocities that attended its conduct of the war remain a subject of hot debate outside of Japan. The emperor's announcement of capitulation, however, led General Douglas MacArthur and his staff to retain him as head of state subject to the decrees of the Supreme Allied Commander in order to ease Japan's transition from a militarist aggressor to a democratic member of the United Nations. As war crimes trials for Japanese officials began, interpreter Shuichi Mizota recalled MacArthur staff member Brigadier General Bonner Fellers telling Admiral Mitsumasa Yonai on March 6, 1946, that: "It would be most convenient if the Japanese side could prove to us that the Emperor is completely blameless. I think the forthcoming trials offer the best opportunity for that. Tojo in particular should be made to bear all responsibility at this trial." When General Hideki Tojo referred to the emperor's ultimate authority during his trial on December 31, 1947, he was subsequently coached to recant that testimony. Renouncing the emperor's incarnate divinity—more to satisfy foreign sentiments than out of personal conviction—Hirohito combined his official reign over a parliamentary Japan with work in marine biology until his death from duodenal cancer on January 7, 1989.

Below: A Mitsubishi G4M1 "Betty" bomber, modified into a 20-seat transport and painted white with green crosses to indicate its purpose, lands on Ie Shima carrying a Japanese surrender delegation on August 19. Escorted to the island by two B-25 Mitchells of the 345th Bomb Group and 12 P-38s of the 49th Fighter Group, the delegates transferred to a C-54 that conveyed them on to Manila to arrange for Allied occupation of Japan.

Opposite: General Douglas MacArthur salutes during an inspection of troops in Manila after the conclusion of meetings with the Japanese surrender delegation on August 20. The Japanese never met or even saw the Supreme Commander of Allied Powers in meetings, which were carried out primarily by MacArthur's chief of staff, Lieutenant General Richard Sutherland. From Manila, the delegates returned by C-54 to Ie Shima and from there to Tokyo in their own planes.

Below: The Allied fleets arrive in Tokyo Bay in preparation for landings at various ports. The first ashore were underwater demolition teams (UDTs) on August 28 to reconnoiter for the safest and best landing locations. Lieutenant Commander Edward P. Clayton, commander of *UDT-21*, landing at Futtsumisaki from the high-speed transport *Burke* (APD-65), became the first to accept a sword in surrender from a major in charge of the local coastal artillery.

Too Little, Too Late

Although aircraft development in the European theater of operations enjoyed greater publicity due to the early use of jet fighters, such as Germany's Messerschmitt Me-262 and Britain's Gloster Meteor, and the rocket-powered Messerschmitt Me-163, the last months of the Pacific War also saw its share of promising and even fantastic aerial weaponry.

A desperate Japan threw up handfuls of excellent fighters, such as the Mitsubishi J2M3 Raiden, Kawanishi N1K2-J, and Kawasaki Ki.100, in quantities too small to matter. It also launched more than 9,000 *Fu-Go* balloons, designed to ride the jet stream across the Pacific and drop bombs on the United States, achieving paltry results—including six civilian deaths—that the US military succeeded in keeping from the public's notice. After the surrender, the Allies discovered that the Japanese were working on a jet fighter and a rocket-powered copy of the Me-163. They had also dispatched new, giant submarines intended to launch the only submarine-based bombers to attack the Panama Canal, only to be recalled before they could be used in action.

The Allies had some new planes of their own, of which the long-range Republic P-47N Thunderbolt fighter and the Consolidated-Vultee B-32 Dominator—a B-29 competitor that saw limited production—were in time to see some combat just before the war ended. Others, such as the Grumman F8F-1 Bearcat carrier-based interceptor, were not, and Britain's jet-powered flying boat fighter, the Saunders-Roe SR.A/1, would not even fly until two years later.

Below: An American examines an Aichi M6A1 *Seiran* ("mountain haze"), a floatplane designed to be launched from giant *I-400*-class submarines and bomb the Panama Canal. One *Seiran* survives at the Udvar-Hazy Center in Chantilly, Virginia.

Left: A Republic P-47N-1-RE of the 1st Squadron, 413th Fighter Group sits on Saipan in mid-1945. With fuel tanks in the wings and square wingtips for a brisker roll rate, the P-47N had a 2,000-mile (3,200km) range that allowed it to escort B-29s.

Below: Having taxied onto a towed landing mat, a Curtiss SC-1 Seahawk with an APS-4 radar pod under the right wing awaits pickup by the battle cruiser *Alaska* off Iwo Jima in March 1945. First flying in February 1944, the Seahawk was the best scouting floatplane the United States produced, but its protracted development delayed its combat use until the Borneo invasion in June 1945, and only 577 were built before the helicopter rendered it obsolete.

Above: A Grumman F8F-1 Bearcat warms up its engine at a Pacific base. Designed as a carrier-based interceptor and boasting a speed of 421 mph (678kph), the Bearcat became operational with VF-19 in May 1945, but the war ended before it could see combat.

Below: Japanese personnel stationed at the Yokosuka Naval Base fall in for the surrender ceremony on August 30, 1945. That morning, Rear Admiral Robert B. Carney, chief of staff of the Third Fleet, arrived with Rear Admiral Oscar C. Badger and Marine Brigadier General William T. Clement aboard the light antiaircraft cruiser *San Diego* (CL-53). Clement led the landing force, which included his 4th Marine Regiment of the 6th Marine Division.

Left: Vice Admiral Michitoro Tozuka, commandant of the Yokosuka Naval Base, is photographed just after surrendering his command to Admiral Carney, the Third Fleet chief of staff, on August 30. General Clement, leader of the shore party, presided over the surrender. In postwar years Yokosuka, located conveniently near Tokyo, has jointly served the US Navy and the Japanese Self-Defense Forces.

Right: MacArthur speaks after the signing of the surrender documents aboard the battleship *Missouri* on September 2, 1945. Representing the Allies behind him are (from left) Admiral Sir Bruce Fraser, Britain, Lieutenant General Kuzma N. Derevyanko, Soviet Union, General Sir Thomas A. Blamey, Australia, General Jacques-Philippe Leclerc de Hauteclocque, France, Vice Admiral Conrad E. L. Helfrich, the Netherlands, and Air Vice Marshal Leonard M. Isitt, New Zealand.

Below: Japanese training aircraft line up at an airfield near Kyoto in September 1945. The Tachikawa Ki.55s in the foreground were training versions of the Ki.36, designed in 1938 and successfully used in the close support role over China. With a total of 1,335 built, both variants were code-named "Ida" by the Allies and, although no match for aerial opposition, they were sometimes sent on suicide missions during the Okinawa campaign.

"Let us pray that peace be now restored to the world and that God will preserve it always. These proceedings are closed."

—*General Douglas MacArthur after the surrender aboard battleship* Missouri, *September 2, 1945.*

Above: Major General Louis E. Woods, commander of the Tactical Air Force, Tenth Army, and Marine Aircraft Wing 2, holds a ceremony on Okinawa, announcing Victory over Japan, or V-J Day, on September 3, 1945. As word of the war's end spread throughout the Pacific, Japanese garrisons stood down, surrendered, and were evacuated home—although handfuls of diehards hid in the caves, hills, and forests for years thereafter.

Left: An honor guard fires a salute at a dedication ceremony at Los Negros Cemetery in 1945. Invaded on February 29, 1944, and secured on May 18, Los Negros in the Admiralty Islands had cost 326 Allied dead and four missing, as well as 3,280 Japanese killed and 75 taken prisoner. Its seizure, however, completed the isolation of Rabaul, Truk, Kavieng, and Hansa Bay, allowing the Allies to move on without invading them.

Hideki Tojo (1884–1948)

Born to an army lieutenant general in Tokyo's Kojimachi District, Hideki Tojo also embarked on a military career, rising to the position of chief of staff to the Kwangtung Army when it invaded China in July 1937. Becoming army minister on July 22, 1940, he supported the tripartite alliance of Japan with Nazi Germany and Fascist Italy. He also negotiated an agreement by Vichy France to allow elements of the Japanese armed forces to operate from French Indochina in July 1941, an act that spurred the United States to impose economic sanctions and an oil and gasoline embargo on Japan.

Gaining the emperor's trust, Tojo became prime minister of Japan on October 18, 1941, and endorsed the decision for "war with the United States, England and Holland" on December 1. His popularity waxed and waned with Japan's military fortunes. After the loss of the Marianas, he resigned as prime minister on July 18, 1944, and went into seclusion.

When General Douglas MacArthur listed him among Japan's 40 primary war criminals and his house was surrounded on September 8, 1945, Tojo shot himself in the chest, but failed to kill himself. After his recovery he was prosecuted at the International Military Tribunal for the Far East in Tokyo, where he is shown giving his deposition on January 6, 1948. On November 18, Tojo was convicted on seven counts of war crimes, and hanged on December 23.

Left: US Navy sailors attached to the Allied occupation forces mingle with the populace of a Japanese city. Although MacArthur's punishment of Japanese war criminals may have been dictated as much by politics as by justice, the overall equity with which the Americans treated the conquered nation paid off with the establishment of a working parliamentary government, good relations between the two nations, and a favorable place for MacArthur in Japanese history books.

Recovery and Rehabilitation

After the loss of one's life, the greatest sacrifice a combatant makes in war is a piece of himself. Of the 599,274 US Army soldiers who were wounded in World War II, 15,000 had limbs amputated. Descriptions of how such casualties were tended to date back to the ancient Greek historian Herodotus, but the state of the art underwent a considerable advance during World War II.

With previous experience predating World War I, Norman Thomas Kirk had literally wrote the book on amputation and prosthetics when he took over the Percy Jones General Hospital in Battle Creek, Michigan, in World War II. There he found his predecessor, Dr. J. Harvey Kellog, removing virtually everything, remarking in exasperation, "When are you coming back for the wallpaper?" Under Kirk's administration, though, its facilities were expanded from caring for 1,750 patients to 12,000. On June 1, 1943, President Franklin Roosevelt appointed Major General Kirk surgeon general, and under his leadership the army's medical corps expanded from 1,500 to a peak of 47,000 physicians, also comprising 57,000 nurses and 1,300 physical therapists.

Most important for amputees was the team approach Kirk devised to deal with them, starting with the premature, temporary closure of the wound, followed by transport stateside to specialized centers for healing, and prosthetic fitting and therapy. The result was an unprecedented improvement in the patients' return to the peacetime world.

Above: A nurse makes necessary adjustments to a prosthetic arm for a soldier patient. The National Academy of Sciences, in coordination with the Veterans Administration, embarked on a research and development program to improve prosthetics.

Above right: WAVE Pharmacist's Mate Third Class Mercedes Palacios works in the pharmaceutical department of the US Naval Hospital at San Diego, California, in the spring of 1945.

Right: Three injured sailors, Shipfitter First Class Steven N. Fecko, Signalman Second Class F. R. English, and Aviation Machinist's Mate First Class L. K. Frendt, exercise under the supervision of Specialist (Auxiliary) Second Class Overton Cheadle at the US Naval Convalescent Hospital at Santa Cruz, California, in June 1945.

Opposite: A navy nurse serves fresh milk, produced at a local Foreign Economics Administration farm project, to injured service personnel convalescing on Guam in June 1945.

Left: A Douglas C-54 takes off from Harmon Field, Guam, in 1945. Operation Magic Carpet, the return of overseas US military personnel, shifted to Asia and the Pacific in October 1945, with 369 navy ships as well as aircraft of the army's Air Transport Command and the Naval Air Transport Service, commandeered toward a repatriation that peaked at 700,000 in December. The Pacific phase of Magic Carpet officially ended in September 1946.

Above: A veteran and his family visit Arlington National Cemetery in Arlington, Virginia, in May 1946. Of 292,131 American military personnel killed in World War II, 106,219 died in Asia and the Pacific. For comparison, Japanese military dead totaled 2,121,955, along with at least half a million civilians. Estimates of Chinese Nationalist army dead vary from three to four million, while Chinese communist partisan and civilian deaths total as high as sixteen million.

Iva Toguri (1916–2006)

No woman who made propaganda broadcasts on Japanese radio ever used the name, but Americans throughout the Pacific came to refer to every seductive voice they heard on the air as "Tokyo Rose." The only broadcaster to be imprisoned for it was born Iva Toguri to Japanese immigrant parents in Los Angeles. In July 1941 she traveled to Japan to visit an ailing relative, but was never issued a passport, and she was still there when the attack on Pearl Harbor occurred. Declared an enemy alien when she refused to renounce her American citizenship, Toguri found work transcribing English-language news broadcasts for the Domei News Agency, then worked for Radio Tokyo. In November 1943 Toguri, often using the name "Orphan Ann," began hosting portions of a show called *Zero Hour*, in which she acted in radio plays and played popular music.

After the Japanese surrender Toguri was arrested in Yokohama on September 5, 1945, held in detention for a year by the US Army, and then released for lack of evidence. The Department of Justice also concluded that her show had been "innocuous." However, popular sentiments in the United States, stirred up by self-serving journalists such as Harry T. Brundidge, Clark Lee, and Walter Winchell, goaded the Federal Bureau of Investigation to renew the investigation. In 1949 she was tried at the US Attorney's Office on eight counts of "overt acts" of treason, convicted of one, fined 10,000 dollars and sentenced to ten years in the Federal Reformatory for Women in Alberson, West Virginia. After six years and two months, she was paroled on January 28, 1956, and moved to Chicago, but remained a noncitizen under the "Tokyo Rose" stigma until 1974, when investigative journalists discovered that two of her Japanese supervisors, under FBI coercion, had lied under oath during the trial. On January 19, 1977, President Gerald R. Ford granted her a full and unconditional pardon, which restored her American citizenship.

"We were in Nuremberg at the GI Olympic stadium when the announcement came. The whole stadium full of guys seemed to rise 20 feet in the air. Nothing could ever compare to a moment like that. It's pretty tough to upstage peace."

—*Bob Hope, on learning of the Japanese surrender.*

Left: In a scene repeated throughout the Pacific and Asia, the 17th Photo Reconnaissance Squadron ceases operations in the wake of V-J Day.

Below: A Japanese flag captured in the Solomon Islands is held up for display from two bayonets in 1945, with the American flag showing through a tear in its center.

Picture Credits

Acknowledgments

Gina McNeely wishes to thank Brooke McNeely for technical assistance.
Jon Guttman wishes to acknowledge the technical assistance from brother Robert Guttman
and colleague Laura Pfost in the course of preparing the text.
Elephant Book Company gratefully acknowledges the Jeff Ethell Collection, www.ww2color.com
and The General Douglas MacArthur Foundation, www.macarthurmemorial.org,
for their kind assistance in the preparation of this book.